"Mother Loyola's name is becoming one that in itself is an endorsement of every book over which it appears...A careful use of Mother Loyola's work will be productive of the best results." --Rosary Magazine, November 1901

About Mother Mary Loyola:

Most Catholics today who have heard the name Mother Mary Loyola know her as the author of *The King of the Golden City*, which has enjoyed a resurgence in popularity in recent years. But few know that she wrote over two dozen works, and that she was once a household name among Catholics of her era. What made her unique among Catholic authors was her ability to draw in her listeners with story after story—and not just any stories, but ones that incorporated current events and brand new inventions of the time. Despite the fact that those events are no longer current, and those inventions no longer brand new, her books scintillate with the appeal of an active mind that could find a moral in the most unusual places. And while the printed word lacks the animated facial expressions and vocal inflections which reveal a gifted storyteller, hers convey her enthusiasm so capably that the reader can easily imagine sitting at the feet of this wise old nun.

About *The Children's Charter*:

Mother Mary Loyola's book *First Communion* had been the gold standard for sacrament preparation for over a decade when the age for reception of this sacrament was lowered in 1910. She then issued this guide for parents and teachers, which reveals just how well she knew the minds of children. They will invariably forget the proper form in the confessional, and their grasp of the more sublime aspects of the gift they are about to receive will not be a firm one. To dwell on rote memorization risks not merely tedium for the children, but an unnecessary fear and avoidance of these sacraments later. Mother Loyola shows that the crucial task is to teach the children a deep love for Our Lord and the proper disposition for receiving Him; this alone can cover many gaps in knowledge, which can easily be filled in later life.

To learn more about Mother Mary Loyola, visit our website at
www.staugustineacademypress.com.

THE CHILDREN'S CHARTER

THE IMPORTANCE OF FAMILY PRAYER

THE CHILDREN'S CHARTER

*Talks with Parents & Teachers
on the Preparation of the Young
for Holy Communion*

BY

MOTHER MARY LOYOLA
OF THE BAR CONVENT, YORK

EDITED BY

REVEREND HERBERT THURSTON, S.J.

2011

ST. AUGUSTINE ACADEMY PRESS
LISLE, ILLINOIS

This book is newly typeset based on the 1911 edition published by Burns & Oates. All editing strictly limited to the correction of errors in the original text, the addition of selected footnotes, and minor clarifications in punctuation or phrasing. Any remaining oddities of spelling or phrasing are as found in the original.

NIHIL OBSTAT:
F. Osmund Cooney, O.F.M.
Provincial

IMPRIMATUR:
Edm. Can. Surmont
Vic. Gen.

WESTMONASTERII,
Die 20 Febr. 1911.

This book was originally published in 1911 by Burns & Oates. This edition ©2011 by St. Augustine Academy Press. All editing by Lisa Bergman.

ISBN: 978-1-936639-05-2
Library of Congress Control Number: 2011941815

To

Christ's Dearly Loved Little Ones

In whose behalf His command has

gone forth afresh:

"Suffer the Little Children to come unto Me

and forbid them not"

CONTENTS

Editor's note:

Mother Mary Loyola's *Children's Charter* is a unique peek into the methods of one of the greatest teachers of Catholic children. In these pages, Mother Loyola sets forth for parents and teachers the crucial points to which they should be attentive when preparing young children for reception of the sacraments.

Of course, being a very humble person, she does not refer the reader to the numerous books she had previously written, which contain in greater depth much of what she touches on here only briefly. So while the current volume might be considered a brief preparatory chat, outlining a sort of "game plan" for educators, much of what the catechist will want for the children themselves to read (or, better yet, *have read to them*) can be found in the following books, also by Mother Loyola:

- *First Confession*, as its title implies, contains much of what is necessary for preparing children for the Sacrament of Penance. Mother Loyola describes the "Four Things" necessary for a good confession in greater detail, amplified with the anecdotes for which she was so famous.
- *Forgive us our Trespasses* is a sort of follow-up to *First Confession*, and can serve as a helpful guide to the many confessions which will hopefully follow the first.
- *First Communion* is the gold standard in preparing children for this Sacrament. Many parents and teachers balk at it because it is a rather thick book. But the contents

of this book are not dry, boring facts to be drilled into the children's heads. (As you will see from reading this book, nothing could be further from Mother Loyola's purpose!) Everything a child needs to know is contained in this volume, written in that inimitable style that made Mother Loyola a household name.

Other titles by Mother Loyola which may be of interest are:

- *The Child of God, or what comes of our Baptism;*
- *Jesus of Nazareth, the Story of His Life, Written for Children;*
- *The King of the Golden City* is an allegory for children which encapsulates a great deal of what Mother Loyola taught about all the sacraments.
- *The Little Children's Prayer Book* also contains many of the suggested prayers found in this volume, in a format suitable for children's daily use.

PREFACE

THE recent decree of the Congregation of the Sacraments regarding the First Communion of children involves one conclusion which is as obvious and incontestable as it is at the same time practically important. The lower the age at which a child is admitted to the holy table, the less he is capable of self-preparation, and consequently the more he becomes dependent upon a teacher's help if he is to "discern the Body of the Lord" as the Apostle and Councils of the Church require. Mother Mary Loyola has fittingly described this decree from the children's point of view as a Charter of privileges. But for teachers, at least, if not for priests, the new legislation can hardly fail to add to their burdens and responsibilities. It seems clear that if our little ones of seven and eight years old are to present themselves at the altar-rails with those sentiments of faith and love which will make their Communions fruitful to their own souls and rich in blessings for the Church in ages yet to come, something more will be required in the teacher than the professional competence which suffices to impart a knowledge of spelling or geography or arithmetic. Undoubtedly God gives special help to work which is undertaken for His sake in a spirit of simple reliance upon His promises. Moreover, we cannot doubt that all the practical bearings of the case were fully weighed by the Holy Father and his advisers before the decree was promulgated.

But it is not difficult to understand that many a teacher may be oppressed by a sense of dismay as she thinks of the difficulty of communicating to her little charges even such a simple desire of the Sacrament and such small measure of comprehension (*aliqualis cognitio*) of its nature as the Holy Father requires by way of preparation.

Under these circumstances this little volume of practical suggestions by a teacher so experienced and successful as Mother Mary Loyola can hardly fail to meet with an enthusiastic welcome. The difficulty here is not one in which profound theologians or erudite historians can help us much. The most indifferently proficient of pupil-teachers probably possesses knowledge enough to suffice—and with a large margin to spare—for the instruction which will now have to be imparted to our First Communion candidates. But it is to the heart of the child, much more than to its intelligence, that the appeal has to be made, and in this matter many a learned priest will be willing to confess that the art of establishing such a *rapport* with a child's deeper consciousness must be learned in the school of practical experience. "An ounce of showing is worth a pound of telling," we are accustomed to say. Mother Loyola cannot transport us all to her school-room and explain the secret of how she manages to catch the attention of the little ones and awaken their love and their enthusiasm for our Lord in the Blessed Sacrament. But readers of the pages which follow will probably agree that so far as the printed word can accomplish it, Mother Loyola has not merely told but shown the imaginary band of inquirers whom she is addressing how they can hope to turn the Children's Communion Charter to account, not only as an incomparable privilege for the little ones themselves, but also as a blessing and a means of grace for those who have the duty of instructing them.

HERBERT THURSTON, S.J.

INTRODUCTION

EVERY day brings home to us with greater force the dangers that await our children when school life is over. And—to judge by the banding together of our forces against irreligion and impiety—we are everywhere awaking to the need of meeting by concerted action the perils ahead.[1]

By the Decree of Pius X, August 8, 1910, the little ones are to be brought to the Holy Table as soon as they come to the use of reason, and on the easiest conditions. The innocence of the child is accounted by the Church its fittest preparation, and the necessity of fortifying the young soul by the presence of Christ lest it "fall into vice before even tasting of the Sacred mysteries" (Decree, August 8), outweighs all considerations that might oppose so early a reception.

Some theologians hold that a child is capable of the dispositions required for Communion before it is ready for Confession, an opinion that will probably be endorsed by many teachers of experience. Be that as it may, the task of preparing children for both Sacraments in the same year will demand all the ingenuity and energy that can be brought to it. For we shall surely not rest content with doing only the absolutely necessary. We shall see in the action of the Church a fresh call for activity

---

1 See "First International Congress of Catholic Women's Leagues"— *The Crucible*, September 28, 1910; and *The Catholic Educational Review*, January 1911,published by the Catholic University of America.

on our part, and do our best to present our little charges at the altar with as fitting a preparation as their tender years permit.[1]

This little book has a threefold object:—

1. To offer to younger and less experienced teachers who have to prepare children for First Confession and First Communion, a few hints as to the matter and method of their instructions.

2. To suggest that First Communicants, young as they will now be, should be encouraged to do something *definite* in preparation for our Lord's visit to them.

3. To urge that on the formation of a First Communion class, every effort should be made to secure the co-operation of mothers and of a helpful influence at home.

The hope throughout has been to quicken zeal, to lessen difficulties, to advocate the adoption of means that promise lasting results.

---

1 "Simple Catechism Lessons," by Dom Lambert Nolle, O.S.B., will be found of great assistance.

PART I
FIRST CONFESSION

I

OUR PRIVILEGES AND
OUR RESPONSIBILITIES

THE two go together always, as light and shade. And nowhere are they more inseparable than in the work of teaching the Christian Doctrine. Whether it be the professor of theology preparing candidates for the Priesthood, or the young teacher in front of her infants, the privilege in the case of both is inestimable. For both is the promise: "They who instruct others unto justice shall shine as stars for all eternity." Because "of all Divine works, the most Divine," according to a maxim ascribed to St. Denis, "is to co-operate with God in the salvation of souls." The Church shows her appreciation of this grandest of works by the grant of an Indulgence each time a lesson in Christian Doctrine is given.

Now for the shade, which, after all, is only beauty in another form. Our responsibilities as teachers equal our privileges. We may not tread heedlessly on holy ground. We must not deal recklessly with souls bought with the Blood of Christ. We have to qualify ourselves for our work, and approach it with the reverence and dependence on God which is the condition of success.

To prepare a child for First Confession and First Communion is an important and delicate task. But the Church is our guide all through. In her divinely controlled action on the souls entrusted to her, there is nothing hesitating or tentative. She knows her work. Deftly and firmly from the first, she handles that mysterious thing, the opening soul of a child, and meets its every need. "Receive this white garment and see thou carry it without spot before the Judgment-seat of God," is her solemn charge to it at the baptismal font. Years pass before she speaks again. But she is waiting and watching. And when, under the action of grace and the various influences brought to bear upon it in home and school life, the ideas of God and of sin have made their way into the consciousness of the child, and rendered it capable at length of grievous offence, when it has come to the use of reason, her voice is heard anew, bidding it examine the white robe, see how far it has been sullied by sin, and bring it to her to be cleansed in its Saviour's Blood. Then she summons it to the altar, and confides to it for its sustenance and safeguard through the journey of life, the greatest of her treasures—the Lord who is to be its companion in the way and at the goal its eternal reward.

Our help here has been offered and accepted. The child has to be brought to the Sacraments. Its conscience must be taught to use them aright. And for this no rough and ready hand will suffice. It is not a task to be got through with as much expedition as possible. Here, surely, if anywhere, the warning words apply: "Cursed is he that doth the work of God negligently."

We see before us row upon row of little faces, unattractive—it may be, unpromising. But behind each is the immortal soul that must be for ever happy or miserable. Each has its crown in Heaven prepared for it; its enemies lying in wait for it. For each the hope of final salvation lies in the Sacraments, and the fruit it will draw from them depends in great measure on our work of preparation.

Do we realise our responsibility, our privilege, our power? Unless we do, we have no business to meddle with the soul of a child. It is too precious to be recklessly or roughly handled. More lasting impressions—so some of our greatest teachers tell us—can be made on the character of a child before it has reached its sixth year than in all subsequent years together. And we have to bear in mind that impressions are made more by what a child sees and feels than by what it hears. We must take ourselves to task then, and ask not only: "Is my grasp of the *matter* to be worked into the child's mind what it should be, but is my *manner* of imparting it such as to make their instructions a delight to the little ones, and my reliance on God such as to draw down a blessing on my work?"

II

Going to Confession

AVING satisfied ourselves that the children know the *Our Father, Hail Mary, I believe, I confess,* what is meant by the Unity and Trinity of God, by the Incarnation, Death, and Resurrection of our Lord, Sin, Heaven, Hell, and Purgatory, we may begin our instructions by taking them to the baptismal font as if to watch a baby's baptism.

Tell them that at Baptism the priest gives the baby a little white robe to show that its soul is clean and beautiful in the sight of God and the holy Angels. Original sin, that ugly mark which would have kept it out of Heaven, is all taken away. And it can never come back. But there is another kind of sin called *actual*, because it was not done by Adam but by our own act and fault. This may come to spoil our beautiful souls and make them worse than ever. It would be a shame to stain our soul when God has been so kind as to wash it clean and make it ready for Heaven. So the priest says to the baby: "Receive this white garment and see thou carry it without stain before the Judgment-seat of God." It is the same as if he said: "Little child, God has made your soul as pure as this white robe. See you do not soil it. He will look at it when you come to Him to be judged. If He should find any big stain on it then, He could not have you with Him in Heaven. He would be obliged to send you far away from Him to a dreadful prison where the punishment never comes to an end—never."

But God does not want to do this, because He loves us very much. We are His dear children, and He wants to take us home to His beautiful Heaven where we shall be happy with Him always. If we do spoil our white soul after Baptism, He is so kind as to wash it again for us and to forgive us. We cannot be baptized again, but He has made another Sacrament to forgive us. This Sacrament we receive when we go to Confession. But—remember this—we are not like the baby at Baptism. It had nothing to do. We have; and unless we do our part we cannot get our sins forgiven.

The Four Things.—We have four things to do to get ready for confession: *First*, we must heartily pray for grace to make a good confession; *second*, we must carefully examine our conscience; *third*, we must take time and care to make a good act of contrition; and *fourth*, we must resolve by the help of God to renounce our sins, and to begin a new life for the future.

1. *I must ask God to help me to make a good Confession.*— The first thing we have to do is to find out our sins. Now, our hearts are dark little places, and often sins hide there in the corners. We cannot see them without light. What do you do when you want to find a thing after dark? You take a light into the room. Only God can take light into your soul and show you the sins that are hidden there. Children who try to find out their sins without asking God to show them where they are, are very silly indeed. God wants to help you to make a good confession. Tell Him you want it very much, and ask Him to help you.

"My God, I want to make a good confession. Please help me, because I cannot do it by myself. Help me to find out my sins and to tell them to the priest. Help me to be sorry for them. Help me not to do them again."

2. *I must carefully examine my Conscience.*—This means I must find out my sins. I can see the naughty things other children do, but perhaps I do not see what I do myself. But God will help me because I have asked Him.

In preparing children for confession, we have to guard against the tendency to give an undue proportion of time to examination of conscience. If they are taught to classify their duties, and to know what come under the headings: (1) to God; (2) to our neighbours; and (3) to ourselves, they will not need to spend much time on this point. Tell them stories of a greedy Freddie, or a sulky Minnie, or an idle Alice, which, by bringing out certain faults, will make examination of conscience easy. The interest they invariably take in the misdoings of other children can be utilised here to any extent. They will really be occupied with examination of conscience whilst you hold up to reprobation the faults of others, as you may gather at times from an approving nod when you happen to strike home, or from a counting off of fingers, or a nudge to a neighbour. Five minutes when they are actually preparing for confession should be enough. It is a great mistake to weary them with a long examination. Keep their minds fresh for what is of far greater importance—sorrow for sin. What can we expect from poor little creatures whom we send into the confessional thoroughly tired out!

Tell them to think of the faults they have found out in their examination of conscience which they ought to make every night before they go to bed; and to put the same kind of faults together: (1) things against God; (2) things against their parents, teachers, and companions; (3) things against themselves. And to think how many times, or about how many times, they have done these things. To take the points in order is to accustom children from the outset to a methodical preparation which, because it makes examination of conscience easy, removes one of the greatest hindrances to frequent confession. We must bear in mind throughout that there is no question of saying all that might be said, but of selecting and carefully adapting to the mind of a child what is essential.

On the subject of examination of conscience our words must be discreet. Pass quickly over the sixth Commandment, taking care in what you say, and in the examination of conscience you may put into their hands, not to bring before their minds anything suggestive of evil. We must ask the Holy Spirit to put the right words upon our lips, that we may say sufficient for the needs of all and not too much for any one in particular.

Though the confession of mortal sin alone is of obligation, we shall do well not to lay too much stress on this; it is better to tell the children to confess whatever sins they remember. Get them to have confidence in the priest. Say we should tell him without fear if anything makes us unhappy. He is there in our Lord's place, so he will always be kind and comforting. He knows all about people's troubles, and will help us and make us happy again directly. He knows all that people have done since the world began, and nothing we can tell will surprise him. He will never be angry with us, and he will never tell any one what we have said, so we need not be afraid; but we must never hide a big sin or tell a lie about it because we were afraid. God would be very angry with us. We should not get any of our sins forgiven; we should be very miserable; and next time we went to confession we should have to tell that sin and that we had hidden it, else it would be told to the whole world at the Last Day. If we do not know how to say something that troubles us, we should tell the priest this when we begin our confession. So we must never leave out anything we think we ought to tell or that makes us unhappy. We should say: "Please, Father, help me to tell something because I am afraid."

If we have tried to examine our conscience properly, and

8

still forget a sin, this is not our fault. It will be forgiven with the rest even if it was a big one. Only, it must be told when we remember it, because every big sin must be confessed once.

It may be worth while to bring in casually two points which may be sources of trouble. A child warned of the sacrilege of hiding a mortal sin through shame might, through a false conscience, be led to commit a sacrilege by hiding what was no sin at all. It may associate natural shame with sin. Take an opportunity of saying that not everything we are ashamed of is a sin. We may blush crimson for having said something that has made us look silly, yet there was nothing wrong in what we are so ashamed of, and there is never anything wrong in what we cannot help.

Difficulty comes sometimes from the particular priest to whom we go to confession. Tell the children that should this happen, we are not obliged to make known to the confessor that what we say concerns himself. "It would be well, when possible," says Cardinal Vaughan,[1] "to give the children a choice of confessors; and especially is it essential not to tire them out by keeping them waiting a long time outside the confessional, and not to let them feel that they are being hurried, or that there is any want of patience or of interest in them."

3. *I must take time and care to make a good act of Contrition.*— God cannot forgive us any sin unless we are sorry. If we said to our father: "I have been disobedient, but I don't care, and I don't mind if I do it again," should we expect him to forgive us? Of course not. And we must not expect God to forgive us unless we are sorry. If we have big sins to confess we must be sorry for every one of them. If we have no big sins, we must be sorry for one at least of the smaller sins which we confess.

What have we to do to get this sorrow? Two things: first, we must ask God to give it us, because we cannot get it by ourselves,

1 *Synodus Diocesana Westmonasteriensis.* Anno 1902, p.19.

and next, we must think of something that will make us sorry.

Some children do not do this. They think that when they have found out their sins, and put them together in little heaps so as not to forget any, they are ready to go to confession. Silly little things! Why, they have left out the chief part of what they have to do. A horse must have his four legs to go anywhere, two or three are not enough. And *we* must have the four things ready to take us to confession whenever we go. And they will not be ready of themselves; we must get them ready. We get sorrow by earnestly praying for it:

> "Dear Jesus, I can do wrong by myself, but I cannot be sorry by myself and make myself good again. Please help me. Make me very sorry for all I have done to displease you."

Any kind of sorrow will not do. If, because we have disobeyed our mother, we are punished by not being taken to the pantomime, we may be very sorry and cry. But this is not the right kind of sorrow when we go to confession. We must be sorry because we have done harm to *our soul* or *to God*.

Do all you can to inspire the children with a fear and hatred of sin—all sin, even the least. Where this solid foundation is not laid, no lasting good can be hoped for; no force is provided against temptation. Show them what an ugly thing sin is—how stealing, telling lies, greediness, are things we are ashamed of. God only forbids us to do what will disgrace and hurt us if we do them.

Tell them mortal sin makes our souls so ugly that we should be frightened if we could see them. Mortal sin changed beautiful angels into ugly devils—changed them in a minute. And it changes our souls too. It makes a soul that was beautiful before quite ugly.

Show them how unjust sin is to God. Utilise the sense of injustice which, in children, is very strong. If some one takes my hat which I bought with my own money and throws it into the mud and spoils it, how angry I am. And what right have I to spoil my beautiful soul which our dear Lord bought with His Precious Blood! Sin is the most dreadful of all things, because it is harm done to the great God who made us. He made all the trees and the flowers, all the bright stars we see over our heads at night. All the men and women in the world are like little grains of sand to Him—He is so great. And He is so kind that He could not be any kinder. Think what it must be to offend a God like this, to be disobedient to Him.

Show them what is lost by one mortal sin—Heaven and the company of Jesus and Mary and the Holy Angels, and all the happy things made ready for us there. God must send any one who dies in mortal sin far away from Him—to hell —for ever. Our Lord always speaks of the punishment of that fearful place as *fire*. He wants to frighten us about hell-fire now when the fear will do us good that we may be afraid of sin, which is the only thing that can take us there. He wants to show us that we must never do anything that would deserve that dreadful punishment, and to be afraid of little sins too, because if we get careless about them we might come to do bigger ones, and because little sins have to be punished in Purgatory where the least pain is worse than anything we can suffer in this world.

Boys and girls—little tiny children, have suffered all kinds of dreadful pain rather than commit sin. Must not we be ready to suffer something, to deny ourselves something? We ought to hate all sin, and the moment we see a thing is wrong, to say: "It would displease God, I won't do it. Jesus and Mary help me." If we do this, we shall be very dear to God and very safe. People who say they will just keep out of mortal sin do not keep out of it. If we let ourselves go right up to the line on the floor when we are playing at oranges and lemons, a big pull will drag us over. If we say to ourselves, "This lie is only a little sin, it does not matter," some day the devil will put a big temptation in our way, and because we have not got the habit of saying "No" to ourselves, we shall not say it then; we shall commit that sin, and—our soul will die!

But of all motives for sorrow, our Lord's Passion is that which appeals most to children. Show them a picture of the Agony in the Garden, or the Scourging, or the Crucifixion. Point out what our dear Lord had to suffer in punishment of our sins, that they may, through compassion for Him, come to have a real hatred and horror of it and put away temptation to mortal sin at once, no matter what the cost may be. Bear in mind that in setting before them scenes of the Passion, it is detail not number that tells. One pain dwelt upon—the burning thirst, the hanging on the wounds, the anguish of His Mother—this makes more impression than many things hurried over. Get them to notice what makes them most sorry, that they may turn to that when they want to make an act of contrition.

We need not think of many things to make us sorry. One is enough, the one we like best. And it need not always be the same.

Sorrow for sin is called *contrition*. The best kind of contrition is to be sorry because God is so good and deserves all the love of our hearts. He loves to see this sorrow in our hearts. He loves us as soon as He sees it there, no matter what sins we have done. He loves us and forgives us even before we go to confession. It is called perfect contrition. Make an act of perfect contrition whenever you have done anything wrong. If you say it with all your heart God will forgive you directly—only, if it was a big sin, you must tell it when you go to confession. Here is an act of perfect contrition:

> "O my God, I am sorry and beg pardon for all my sins, and detest them above all things, because they deserve Thy dreadful punishments—because they have crucified my loving Saviour Jesus Christ, *and, most of all, because they offend Thine infinite goodness.*"

It is not hard to get this best sorrow. God will always give it to us it we ask Him properly. Our dear Lord loved to forgive sin when He was living here on earth. He loved to say: "Thy sins are forgiven thee," and to send people away quite happy. But what was He to do when He went back to Heaven? He knew that we too should want to have our sins forgiven, so He gave His priests the same power He had Himself. We are to go to them as we should have gone to Him. He has promised to forgive what they forgive. When the priest says: "I absolve thee from thy sins in the name of the Father, and of the Son, and of the Holy Ghost," God forgives what His priest forgives—if we have done our part.

And now we must understand this. It happens very often that when we have tried to make a good act of contrition we do not *feel* sorry, and so we think we are not sorry. A boy said to a priest: "I know I was sorry when my mother died. I cried all night. But I have never cried for my sins, so I can't be really sorry for them." This boy made a mistake. He felt very sorry when he heard of his mother's death, and he cried bitterly. But there can be real sorrow without tears. Sorrow is not in our eyes but in our heart. If we say as well as we can: "I am sorry for what I have done; I wish I had not done it; with God's help I will try not to do it again"—we are really sorry.

Notice these last words: "I will try not to do it again." We always say this when we ask our father or mother to forgive us; God expects us to say it to Him, and to mean what we say. He does not expect we shall never do any of these things again, but only that we will try not to do them. And so the last of the four things we have to see to when we go to confession is a purpose of amendment.

4. *I must renounce my sins and begin a new life for the future.*—What do we do when we have fallen several times in the same place? We look back to see what it was made us slip

there. Was it a piece of orange-peel? Or had boys been making a slide? We look back to find out what it was, that we may not fall there again.

We must look back now. We must think of the chief faults we are going to tell in confession. In what places did we fall into those faults? Was it in church, or in the school, or in the play-ground, or when we were alone? We must think how we can prevent falling again in that place. We must say: "What is the worst thing I am going to say in confession? Or what have I done oftenest? And what must I do to be better?"

If I say my prayers carelessly at home or in church, looking about all the time, I will remember when I kneel down that God is looking at me to see how I am going to speak to Him. When thoughts of play or other things come, I will try to send them away as soon as I notice them. If I do wrong by going with a companion who does wrong, I will ask the priest what I must do. I will pick out one fault that I will try most of all not to do again, and say: "With God's help, I will try to be better in this. At least I will try not to do it so many times."

What should greedy Freddie make up his mind to do? And sulky Minnie? And lazy Alice? What they make up their mind to do is called their good resolution or *purpose of amendment*.

What is *my* resolution to be about? I could advise all these children wisely; I must advise myself. I must not say: "I am going to be quite good now and never naughty any more." That is a silly resolution which will not do any good. But if I have been lazy and say: "I will jump up the minute I am called. I will ask mother what I can do to help her, and I will try to be useful in the house"—this is a good resolution.

It is better to make a purpose of amendment about one or two things than about many things. And it is good to ask our Lord what He would like best. We shall soon find out what He wants, for He will whisper it gently in our heart. A little child said: "I shut my eyes and then I hear the little voice. He told me yesterday that if I was a better girl, father would not look at me like that."

Try to arrange that the children shall not have long to wait for their turn. Wait with them, and when they are ready find them some prayers to say or some pictures to look at, *e.g.* the Stations of the Cross. When it is near their time to go in, bid them think again what sins they are going to tell that they may have them quite ready. Then tell them to make an act of contrition for all these sins and for one in particular, the one they are most sorry for.

To make sure of their contrition in every confession, it is well to advise them to tell some sin of their past life, already confessed, for which they know they are sorry, and to make an act of contrition for it before they go into the confessional.

Perhaps some questions on the ground we have gone over may be of use—

QUESTIONS

- What did the priest give us when we were baptized? Why did he give it?
- What did he say to us when he gave it?
- What would spoil our white soul after baptism?
- Why do we go to confession?
- How many things have we to do to get ready tor confession?

1. Why must we ask God to help us to find out our sins?
   - Who can say a prayer to ask His help?

2. What is the second thing we have to do?
   - What does examination of conscience mean?
   - Do we examine our conscience only when we are going to confession?

- How can we put our faults together so as to remember them?
- What kind of sins are we obliged to tell in confession?
- If we are not sure that something was a sin, or if we are unhappy about something, what should we do?
- Why must we never be afraid to tell the priest if we are in trouble?
- What may we say if we do not know how to tell a sin?
- What would happen if we were to hide a big sin or to tell a lie about it?
- If we had tried to examine our conscience properly and still forgot a big sin?

3. Which of the four things we have to do is the most important?
   - Will any kind of sorrow do when we go to confession?
   - How can we get the right kind of sorrow?
   - Must we do anything to get it besides asking God for it?
   - What things can we think about that will make us sorry?
   - What will you think about?—and you?— and you?
   - Why must we hate sin so much?
   - What does mortal sin do to the soul?
   - What would happen to any one who died in mortal sin?
   - What should we do when we are tempted to sin?
   - Why must we be afraid of little sins?
   - May we say: "I will tell this lie, it is only a little sin?"
   - Where do people go who have venial sins on their souls when they die?
   - How can we get our sins forgiven?
   - If we had done a big sin could we get it forgiven before we went to confession?
   - Who can make an act of perfect contrition?
   - Can we be really sorry for our sins if we do not *feel* very sorry?
   - What is absolution?

4. What is the fourth thing we have to do when we go to confession?

- What is a purpose of amendment? Another name for it?
- Should we all make the same resolution?
- What should a disobedient child make? A quarrelsome one? A lazy one?
- What did a child do who wanted to know what would be a good resolution to make?

In the Confessional.—Satisfy yourself that the children know well the form of confession. It is marvellous how utterly at sea they can be even after careful instruction. They will go in and say: "Please, Father, I give you my blessing," or a Hail Mary, as the beginning and end of their confession.

Tell them when the priest says in Latin the words of absolution to bow down their head and say: "My God, I am sorry for all my sins because you are so good." Or, better still perhaps, the long act of contrition: "O my God, I am sorry and beg pardon for all my sins, and detest them above all things, &c." Some priests who like this to be said aloud in order to secure it, find it impossible to get the children to say it.

Teach them to be sure to remember the penance given them. If they do not hear what the priest says, or do not know the prayer he gives them to say, they must tell him. Tell them they should *say* their penance, *i.e.* recite it with their lips, not simply read it.

When they come out of the confessional they should go to their place with their eyes cast down.

Thanksgiving after Confession.—We are very happy now and thank God with all our heart for making our soul so white and beautiful. We say some prayers in thanksgiving, and then we say our penance. This is very short and easy. But if we say it well, it will take away a great deal of the punishment we have deserved by our sins. We should say it with our lips, not just read it with our eyes.

If the priest has told us to do anything; if we have to give back something we have taken, or to unsay something untrue we said about somebody, we should think how soon we can do this.

We tell our Lord again what that fault is we are going to fight and we ask Him to help us. We shall not mend all at once. We shall have to try hard, and often we shall break our good resolution and do the bad things again. But we must never give up. "Try, try, try again," we must say to ourselves. Even the best people break their good resolutions many and many a time. But who succeed in the end? Not those who tried most the first day or two and then gave up, but those who go on and on, who are sorry when they break their resolution, and then try again as if they had never broken it. This is very brave. We will do this. If we like, we may pay a visit to our Lady's altar and put our resolutions into her keeping.

Our Confessions.—We must go to confession as often as the priest has told us, and not put off without real need. And we must always remember two things whenever we go to confession:—

1.   Never to go in a hurry and before we have had time to do the four things;

2.   Never to go into the confessional till our act of contrition has been properly made.

It is most important that a child's first experience of spiritual things should be a happy one. The matters with which we have been dealing—sin and its punishment, examination of conscience, confession, &c.—are not in themselves entertaining. To make them even tolerable to the children, all the resources of our ingenuity will be required. Illustration, abundant and varied, must come to our help throughout. Its concreteness arouses the child's interest and calls forth its remarks. These furnish a clue to its mind and enable us to discover how far we have made ourselves understood. "The concrete," says Cardinal Vaughan, "is the way to get at their understanding, not the abstract." No good will be done unless the children follow us with pleasure. If you see attention flagging have recourse at once to illustration. Seize hold of anything that enters within the sphere of their experience or interest. They love animals: weave in some curious story of a dog or a monkey that, with a little stretching, can be brought to bear upon the subject. We should always have our eyes open and our tentacles feeling about for anything that will add to our store of illustration. You may fall back upon their games or upon some little event that has made a stir in home or school life and is uppermost in their thoughts at the moment. Inattention shows you have lost touch with their mind. You must catch some vehicle to bring you up with it again. Do not blame them for wandering after something more interesting than you are, but make yourself so interesting that there is no temptation to wander. And be short. Ten minutes or a quarter of an hour at a time is as long as we can expect to fix the thoughts of little children on such subjects as we want to drive home. We must beware lest by length or by heaviness, by regarding their instructions as a lesson that has to be learnt, or by exacting too much of them, we create weariness or disgust, and thus lose all the fruits we hope for.

In any instruction, in any story you tell them, do not let them catch you reading. "Tell us about it," is their constant pleading. All the charm is gone when your eyes are lowered upon your book. The *matter* is only half of what is essential. In dealing with little children, so sensitive to outward impressions and so helpless in our hands, the greatest attention must be given to our *manner*. Our eyes, our expression, the tone of our voice, our way of speaking, animated or otherwise—these are the book in which they read, and whether we will or no. We carry them along with us if we are bright and animated—but *we must talk*. No book language, no speech of another is simple enough, intimate enough, living enough to bring us into the close contact that is wanted with their intelligence, heart, and will. We must assimilate everything, make it part of ourselves, before we give it to them. And then, to the eager eyes and ears before us, we must show and tell it all—*we must talk*.

We must be very patient, too, and content with little, bearing in mind not merely the weakness of the child's powers, only just beginning to exert themselves, but also the abstract nature of the matters in which we are seeking to interest them. Whilst making use of all expedients our ingenuity can devise to arrest attention and secure interest for our subject, we must beware of over-eagerness, and of expecting to see much in the way of results. If our lesson is well thought out and brightened with familiar illustrations, more will sink in than we are aware of, and for the very reason that it sinks in, it will not appear just yet. Wait. Give it time. When and where we least expect, we shall find the seed has sprung up and brought forth fruit, thirty, sixty, and a hundredfold.

PART II

FIRST COMMUNION

III
WE ASK OURSELVES A QUESTION

WHEN we speak of preparing our children for First Communion, we know of course that the Sacrament works by its own efficacy. But this in no way dispenses with the most careful preparation of mind and heart, "For grace does not work miracles; at least we have no right to expect that it will; and whenever human and natural agency has its sphere of work such agency must be given. God giveth the increase, but, for all that, Paul must plant and Apollo must water...Children who are hurriedly brought to their first Communion, without training in piety and without seemly habits, are but little affected by the reception of their Saviour's body. The impression quickly fades from their minds; they remain in their forlorn state; too often they never come back to the Sacraments; and they grow up, as temptation makes itself felt, to that life of sin and degradation for which their childhood was the preparation and of which it was the prophecy...What they lose by not being prepared for their first Communion, they hardly ever recover in after life. For they rarely learn to make the Holy Communion their daily bread; they seldom acquire that habit of regularly approaching the Sacrament, without which, it may be said, it is impossible to avoid mortal sin. Hence it is not too much to say that the greater number of those who neglect the Sacraments, owe this fatal indifference to the way in which they made their first Communion..."[1]

The natural question that strikes us on reading these weighty words is:—Are we doing all we can to secure the needful preparation of mind and heart? Much is expected, and rightly expected, of children at this momentous period of their lives, much during the time of preparation, much in after fruits. Does the help we provide for them bear any proportion to our expectations? What provision are we going to make *now* to secure for the very little ones coming up to the altar the necessary preparation of mind and heart?

By the Catechism of the Council of Trent (Part II, par. 63) two qualities are required in a child before it is admitted to First Communion—knowledge and desire. The knowledge required is the very least that could be exacted—"that the child should understand according to its capacity those chief doctrines of faith without which there is no Christianity; that is to say, that there is a God, that God loves us, that He rewards the good and punishes the wicked, that the Father, the Son, and the Holy Ghost are equally God, though there is only one God, and that the Son of God became man and died to redeem us. Add to this, that there must be some recognition of what the Blessed Sacrament is; that is to say, that it is not common bread, but something holy, bringing Jesus into our soul. It is evident that it is quite possible to teach these things in an informal way to a child of seven...But it must always be remembered that children differ in capacity, and that there are some who can take in very little indeed."[2]

Desire, that is, relish, or spiritual feeling, must depend in

---

1   Pastoral Letter of the Right Rev. Bishop Hedley for Lent, 1893.
2   Pastoral Letter for Advent, 1910 —Bishop Hedley.

great measure on the way in which we set about the work of preparation. That this presents many difficulties especially at first, and with all the disadvantages under which we labour, cannot be denied. But obstacles must not discourage us or make us drive through our work as if it were a task. That would be fatal to the end we have in view. If the poor babies come to look upon their instruction only as one lesson more in the day, what chance has Desire of finding its way into their hearts? We must do all we can to make it a joyous time, a time they look forward to, a time bright with stories, with pictures if we can get them, and with some simple hymns that they can understand.

Teachers, children, mothers—all these should share in the great work before us, and know clearly from the outset in what it consists. Let us consider, then:

(1) The aim to be set before teachers, with some helps to attain it.

(2) The preparation to be proposed to the children themselves.

(3) The co-operation that may be reasonably expected of mothers.

Our work as teachers is to lead the child up to our Blessed Lord, that it may see and hear and touch Him, that His influence may pour in upon its soul through every avenue, that it may come to the altar-rails—not with a few dry dogmas as its sole provision, but with the eager desire that can say: "I know in whom I have believed."

Obviously, the only way to do this is to make the children familiar with His life, with such portions and incidents in particular as most appeal to them, and to set these before them in an attractive manner. The task is not an easy one. The bulk of our children can do little by themselves. Even when dealing with objects that appeal to eye and ear and hand, we must have recourse to all manner of expedients to arrest their attention and gain their co-operation. How much more is this the case when the subject-matter is beyond the reach of sense, and when concentration of mind and effort of will are claimed at times for things distasteful to the best disposed?

How can we bring within the range of their imagination and intelligence and heart and will the truths we want them to grasp with a grip that will last through life? Only by realising that we must appeal to every one of these faculties and make a distinct study of the road to each. Imagination and intelligence we may take together. Through the first we shall reach the second. "Truth," says Cardinal Newman, "is poured into the mind of the scholar by his eyes and ears, through his affections, imagination, and reason...and is sealed up there In perpetuity."[1]

"It has been intended that we should all learn, children especially, through the senses, with which God has enriched our nature."[2]

To enable the life and actions, the words and personality of our Lord to impress themselves upon the imagination of the children, we may take them to the cottage of Nazareth, to the Temple, through the streets of Jerusalem, on to the stormy lake or the grassy plain, letting them see Him among the poor and the sick and the little ones, feeding the multitude, seated at table with the Twelve. We can paint all this in vivid colours so that there shall not be a wandering eye or a careless listener before us. Children are not flatterers. If we bore them, they will let us know it. Watch the tell-tale faces. These and their questions and answers are our best guide as to what appeals to them.[3]

---

1   "Historical Sketches," iii., p. 14.
2   Lenten Letter on the Religious Training of Children. Their Preparation for First Communion—Cardinal Vaughan.
3   Much in this and the succeeding chapters has already appeared in the author's paper on First Communion, written for the Eucharistic Congress, Montreal.

Many of us will perhaps urge that there is no opportunity in the already over-crowded day, and, amid the crush of Government subjects, for such elaborate preparation, no leisure on the part of the teacher, no time for such instruction. But could we not anticipate the work in the preceding Standards? Surely our Lord's Life is of greater interest than Abraham's, and the obedience of the Child Jesus at Nazareth more to the point than the jealousy and cruelty of Joseph's brethren!

The demand on the teacher's scanty leisure is certainly a difficulty, and one so deserving of sympathy, that a fellow-teacher has tried to lessen it by bringing together the main points of the important work now on hand and indicating the simple books of reference available for fuller information.

IV
THE LIFE OF OUR LORD

This must be the backbone of our instruction from first to last. The aim of our Holy Father Pius X is to save society by "restoring all things in Christ." Ours is a sweeter task—to win for Christ at the outset those innocent souls which the world has not yet spoiled. They have not, thank God, to be "restored," but led up to Him in their freshness. They have to be brought with the first dawn of reason under the spell of His attractiveness; and it is our privilege to present them to Him.

It would be well for us to make out a scheme of instruction, selecting, according to the time at our disposal, the incidents in the Gospels bearing more directly on our subject. These should be set before the children, one only at each lesson, in vivid word pictures. If we can also have a pictorial representation of the scene, so much the better. And as for such pictures and for the questions arising from them a certain sense of leisure is required, it might be advisable, as has been suggested, to anticipate our work in the preceding Standards.

If they have learned anything of Old Testament History, we ought not to have more to do now than to refresh the memory of what they already know. After touching briefly on the Creation and Fall of our first Parents, and on the Promise of a Redeemer who was to reopen to us the gates of Heaven, we may go straight to His Coming and to the early scenes of His Life. These, if well described, always interest children, and are invaluable for the lessons they teach.[1] The Holy House of Nazareth, the school of meekness, humility, and obedience; the streets, hillsides, seashore of Judea and Galilee where our Lord "went about doing good"; the gloomy desert where He was tempted; the flowery plain where He fed the five thousand; the Synagogue of Capharnaum where He gave the promise of the Eucharist; the Supper Room on Mount Sion where He said the first Mass and ordained the first priests—all these we may show in a way that perhaps for life will impress upon imagination, mind, and heart the Personality of our Divine Lord, and win for Him now the innocent hearts whose love He covets.

At the risk of being wearisome we must repeat it—take pains to make all your stories attractive. Put in the bright touches, the bits of detail that children love. It means real labour, enthusiasm, zeal, personal love of our Lord. But He looks to us for all this. We are His apostles. He follows with keenest interest our every look and word and gesture. If we ask Him He will direct all these to the end we have in view. Through our means He will draw to Himself the hearts of these little ones, and be our "reward exceeding great."

No one of any experience in teaching could seek to minimise the labour involved in the work of religious instruction. "It is difficult," said Cardinal Vaughan to his clergy, "for ordinary teachers, wearied by continuous work at the Government subjects, to bring that freshness and devotion to the teaching of religion which are so important in order to win the affection of the children to God and to the Church." It is difficult, yet

1   If time and the capacity of the children permit, it may be advisable to add instructions on the Paschal lamb, the Sacrifice of Melchisedech, the Manna in the Desert, and the Prophecy of Malachias—those foreshadowings of the bloody and unbloody Sacrifice to come.

we have to try to learn "the art of so speaking as to rivet the attention of the young."[1]

A priest of much experience tells us that the idea of Holy Communion which appeals most to children is that of our Lady laying her little Babe in their arms for them to take care of and to love. The marriage feast at Cana, the storm on the lake, the blessing of little children, are scenes that always interest them. In all you say seek to draw their hearts to our Lord. Dwell not only on His marvellous works, but on the gentle majesty of His face, the charm of His voice, His tender words and winning ways, the sweetness of His smile, the grace of His every movement, that attracted all hearts and won Him not admiration and reverence only, but love. Tell them how the reaper threw aside his sickle, the carpenter his saw, how women laid down their distaff, caught up their babes, and hurried forth to join the crowd that was gone after Jesus of Nazareth. How the poor sick were laid in their beds where He was to pass, or carried up and down hill after Him right out into the desert where He had gone to seek a little rest. How the blind, the deaf, the lepers pressed round Him wherever He went, and everywhere the children were His bodyguard, crowding about Him to see the cures. How the officers sent to take Him were held spell-bound like the rest, and went away saying: "Never man spake like this Man."

Tell them of His kindness to the widow who had lost her only son, to the children whom the disciples would have driven from Him, to the father and mother who brought Him where their little daughter of twelve lay dead on her bed, to the sinner who was not afraid to press His sacred feet with her lips. Make it all real to them. Make Him live and move before them. Let them fall in love with His beautiful character as seen in His words and ways. Paint a picture of Him in their minds which

1   "Life of Cardinal Vaughan," p. 390—J.G. Snead-Cox.

will last through life and keep them loyal to Him, or win them back should they go astray.

Tell them, and keep reminding them that this dear Lord whom they would have loved and run after like the Jewish children, had they known Him when He was living upon earth, *is our God*, the God whom we have to adore; that He is coming *to them* as really as He went to Martha and Mary, and that He looks for a welcome from His little First Communicants as He did from His friends at Bethany who loved Him so dearly.

A great help here would he the occasional use of lantern slides, representing scenes from the life of our Lord, those especially having reference to the Blessed Sacrament. A selection of slides could easily be made, and supplemented by suitable subjects from the lives of the Saints, and of the infant lovers of Jesus in the Eucharist our own days have seen. In France, Belgium, and Spain diocesan associations exist for utilising the cinematograph, accompanied by catechetical teaching, as a means of religious instruction,[1] thus representing to the eyes of children not the form only but the movement which will make the Gospel scenes live before them. Think of their delight could they see the Jewish children not only crowding round our Lord, but being actually taken up into His arms and embraced and blessed, and nestling on His breast! Would not this bring home to them the Eucharistic embrace for which they are preparing? Or they might watch the Blessed Mother laying her Divine Child in the arms of a little child, and so realise something of the Trust to be confided to themselves. In the same way they might make acquaintance with the peasant child of six in converse with St. Alphonsus, who allows her the privilege of making her First Communion at that early age.

1 Information on the subject can he obtained at the General Secretariat, Rue Jourdan, Brussels. The Maison de la *Bonne Presse*, 5 Rue Bayard, Paris, has a large assortment of religious slides. Its catalogue can be had on application.

To obtain satisfactory results in this way would involve labour and expense. Undoubtedly, and it is only at this cost they have been secured abroad. Could we not profit by what has been already done, and make some generous effort when there is question of presenting the little ones to our Lord as happy and as eager as we can? We must be ingenious, resourceful, enterprising. We must try one scheme after another, interchanging ideas, comparing results. If one suggestion is found impracticable, let us cast about for something else.

Hymns are another help. Children love hymns and learn them easily. Their own resources before and after Communion are soon exhausted. A few simple rhymes containing no ideas that cannot be easily grasped by all in the class prove very useful.[1]

---

1 The author desires to express her obligations to a Sister of Notre Dame for the Communion verses that follow.

V

THE BREAD FROM HEAVEN

When you come to the feeding of the five thousand in the desert, as narrated in the sixth chapter of St. John, you have reached an event which you must strive to make specially interesting to your class, for it brings before them a most remarkable type of the Holy Eucharist, and was immediately followed by the promise of the Bread of Life.

Tell the children that they have seen how our Lord loved us when He was on earth. Because He loved us He came all the way from Heaven to save us from sin and hell:

> All the way from highest bliss
> Down to such a world as this.

For thirty-three years He gave us His life as an example. He lived as a poor man, working for His daily bread. He showed us how to bear hunger, cold, weariness, unkindness, affronts. He died for us upon the cross. Then He rose again from the dead, and after forty days went up to Heaven to open its gates for us.

He was always thinking of us because He loves us so. Now, when friends love each other very dearly, they want to be always together. If one has to go away, there are letters, photographs, keepsakes of many kinds to remind them of one another. Our Lord is our best Friend. He had to go away from us at the

Ascension. But He could not bear to go altogether. He wanted to stay with us to help us to be good, and to get to Heaven. He wanted not only to be near us, but even to come into our souls that He might be able to help us more. So He made a way of staying really with us, though we cannot see Him. He hides Himself beneath the appearances of a little bread, as if behind a curtain, that He may come into our souls and feed us with Himself.

This is so wonderful that when He first spoke of it He had to try to make it as easy as He could for the people to believe. He worked a great miracle which we are going to think about now.

1. *The Feast in the Desert.*—Put the scene in the desert vividly before the children—the multitude, five thousand men, besides women and children, making bright patches of colour like flower-beds on the grass; our Lord, standing on the rising ground with His Apostles round Him, taking the bread, blessing it, giving it for distribution to the Twelve. He is thinking of another Feast, another Bread, other ministers, other men, women, and children, to be fed not once only, but as often as they will with the Bread from Heaven which He is going to give them.

2. *The Promise of the Eucharist.*—Take the children to the synagogue of Capharnaum, where, the day after the miracle, the first instruction on the Holy Eucharist was given and the Twelve were prepared for their First Communion.

Picture the scene:—

(1) The eager listeners, full of the miracle of the day before, thinking of nothing else, talking of nothing else but the wonderful bread, wanting more of it; every eye fixed on our Lord; the breathless silence when He began to speak.

(2) Our Lord's promise to give them a better Bread—a Bread from Heaven. This Bread will be Himself, the Bread of Life, to keep their souls alive, that they may not die by mortal sin.

(3) Those who eat this Bread shall live for ever.

(4) This bread will be His Flesh, which He will give for the life of the world.

(5) The Jews ask: "How can this Man give us His flesh to eat?"

(6) Our Lord's answer: Unless you eat the Flesh of the Son of Man and drink His Blood you shall not have life in you."

(7) They complain: "This is a hard saying," and many leave Him.

(8) "Will you also go away?" our Lord asks of the Twelve. Peter's answer. Point out that our Lord did not call them back to say they had mistaken His meaning. He really meant what He said. He did not want them to *understand* but to *believe*. After the wonders they had seen Him do, they ought to have believed. His Twelve Apostles stood round Him, thoughtful, reverent, silent. They did not understand, but they knew He could do all things, and they believed. They taught others what they believed, and their faith has come down to us—that in the Blessed Sacrament Jesus Christ is really and truly present— Body, Blood, Soul, and Divinity—hidden under the appearance of Bread. Let us say with faith and with love: "Lord, give us always this Bread!"

If the children can follow you, you might show the points of resemblance between the Divine Bread and the bread given in the desert. But never overtax them; better a thousand times to leave your story incomplete than to weary them with what they cannot take in.

1. The Bread from Heaven is our Lord's own Feast, prepared by Himself!

2. It is given in the desert.

3. To all His followers, even His children followers.

4. To those who hunger for it.

5. It is multiplied to satisfy all.

6. It is distributed not by Himself, but by His ministers.

7. It is a delightful Food, giving strength and gladness.
8. It makes those who receive it know Him and love Him.

3. *The Last Supper.*—Picture the scene—the low table, the couches round, the washing of the feet, the announcement of the betrayal. Our Lord, as He takes the bread into His holy and venerable hands, and lifting His eyes to Heaven, gives thanks, and blesses, and breaks, and says: "Take ye and eat. This is My body. This do for a commemoration of Me." It was the first Mass, the first Consecration, the first change of bread into His sacred Body. The First Communicants were fed with the true Bread from Heaven. The first Priests were ordained.

They did not understand even now, but they believed and adored. Then came the Consecration of the chalice: "Drink ye all of this, for this is My Blood of the New Testament which shall be shed, &c." Again, They received what He gave them—His true Blood under the appearance of wine. This wondrous change takes place at the Consecration in every Mass. How reverent, how attentive we ought to be!

Our Lord gave the Apostles power to do what He had done—to change bread into His Body and wine into His Blood, and to pass on this power to the priests of His Church to the end of the world, that all who believe in Him, all His little children, may receive Him into their hearts, and be taken by Him to Heaven some day. There, as a reward of their faith now, they will see Him face to face.

This was the Keepsake He left us—Himself—to remind us of Him. And so He said to His dear Apostles that night when He gave it: "Do this for a commemoration of Me." When we receive Him into our hearts He likes us to think of Him and of all He has done for us, so think of His bitter death for us, and to thank Him for the wonderful Keepsake He left us before He went away.

Of the three chief dogmas respecting the Blessed Sacrament,

see that the children know (1) that our Lord is really present in the Sacred Host, and (2) that He comes there when the priest says the words of Consecration at Mass. That He is whole and entire in each of the species and in every part of the species, would probably only puzzle them now. Yet their quaint and often beautiful fancies which now and again come to light, show that these small "faithful" take in more than we suppose. A child of eight thinks that our Lord in His visible Human Nature is always in the Tabernacle, but "changes," i.e. slips into His disguise when the priest opens the Tabernacle door. "I watch to see Him change," she says, "but He is too quick." So here are our Lord and His little servant playing at hide-and-seek every Sunday at Mass!

Tell the children how pleased our Lord is when we believe what He tells us, *because He has said it*, though we cannot understand. How the angels bow down before the Tabernacle and fill the Sanctuary at Mass. How St. Louis of France would not go to see a miracle at Mass—a beautiful Babe in the priest's hands after the Consecration. "I believe," he said, "I do not want to see yet. I would rather have our Lord's blessing on those who have not seen and have believed." Whenever we genuflect reverently before the altar or make an act of faith, we please our dear Lord. But we must show we believe when we are in church. What do the angels think of children who say: "My God, I believe that You are really present on the altar," and then talk or laugh, or try to distract others?

Tell the children stories that will show them the desire of children for Holy Communion.

1. Blessed Imelda, a little Italian child, longed to receive Jesus into her heart with the other children of Bologna who, on the Easter Sunday of the year 1393, were to make their First Communion. But she was considered too young and had to

remain in her place when they went up to the altar. Was she to be disappointed then? No. One was there who did not think her too young. He saw that little longing heart, and His Heart was longing too. When the priest turned to the communicants and holding the Blessed Sacrament, said: "Behold the Lamb of God," the Sacred Host left his hand, and, passing down the church, remained in the air over the head of Imelda. The priest saw in this miracle the desire of our Lord, and going to the place where the child was kneeling, satisfied the great God of Heaven and that little eager heart. It was her First and Last Communion. She was so happy that she died of joy whilst thanking her Lord for this loving visit, and went to see Him face to face, and be happy with Him for ever.

2. Over a hundred years ago there was a little mite, only four, who longed to receive Holy Communion as soon as she heard that Jesus is really present in the Blessed Sacrament. She used to ask every priest she met to give her our dear Lord, but the answer was always the same—she was too young and must wait. At last she found a priest who gave her Holy Communion and filled her with joy. But she was not content with receiving our Lord once only: she wanted to have Him with her again and again, and she contrived a way for satisfying her desire. There was a holy old man then living in Naples—St. Alphonsus Liguori. She coaxed her aunt to take her to see him, and the two were left in conversation together—the old man of nearly ninety and the child of four. He was glad to hear of her First Communion, and said she might go again and often, and he told her to love our Lord with all her heart and to pray for sinners.

3. In May, 1907, a little child of four was in the Industrial School at the Convent of the Good Shepherd, Cork, Ireland. She was ill and suffered much. One day her nurse carried her

down to the convent chapel where the Blessed Sacrament was exposed, and told the little one as she sat beside her, Who it was that was there in the midst of the lights and flowers, and that "Holy God" had come all the way from Heaven to show His love to us. From that time the child's love of our Lord in the Blessed Sacrament was truly wonderful. She seemed to understand as few of us do the love of Jesus for us. On Exposition days, though no one told her of them, she always begged nurse to take her down to "Holy God." There she would remain, quiet and content, her eyes fixed on the monstrance, her little hands joined in prayer. Her longing to receive the Blessed Sacrament grew more and more, and at last she was allowed to make her First Communion. As soon as she woke that morning Nellie begged nurse to be quiet and get everything ready, "for you know," she said, "Holy God is coming." From that time till her death in 1908 she received Holy Communion nearly every day. It was touching to see the effort she made to bear her pain patiently. Often her sufferings were intense, but when any one pitied her she would say: "Our Lord suffered more than this."

Dwell on the lessons taught by these baby lovers of our Lord. Show how the faith in their hearts made them want to be with Him, made them behave well in church, bear patiently things they did not like, things that hurt, &c.

Reverence must not degenerate into dread and fear. The bulk of their instructions should inspire a joyous desire for their First Communion. Yet we shall do well not to omit that one lesson of warning given by our Lord Himself—with all His desire to be with us—the parable of the Wedding Garment. This will lead us to speak again of Confession, a subject which should be frequently reviewed, and at this time especially when it is important to satisfy ourselves that all are sufficiently instructed and know how to prepare for it.

40

QUESTIONS

1. Who can tell us about the Feast in the Desert?
2. Did our Lord ever promise the people a better bread than He gave them there?
3. What was this Bread to be?
4. Why does He give us this holy Bread?
5. What will happen to our souls if we do not eat this Bread?
6. What do we call this holy Bread?
7. When did our Lord make this Blessed Sacrament?
8. What did He do at the Last Supper to show how clean our souls ought to before Holy Communion?
9. What are the words by which our Lord changed bread into His Sacred Body, and wine into His Blood?
10. Does that change ever happen now? When?
11. How do we know at Mass when that great change is being made?
12. How should we behave at this time?
13. Is there any bread in the priest's hand after he has said the words of Consecration?
14. What does "Consecration" mean?
15. What should we do when the priest lifts up the Sacred Host?
16. Why does the bell ring?
17. Why does our Lord come down upon the altar at Mass?
18. What do we mean by the Real Presence?
19. Why do we believe in the Real Presence?
20. Who knows the story of St. Louis at Mass?
21. Why did our Lord come to little Imelda?
22. Why did little Nellie long so much to go to Holy Communion?

VI

THE VISIT OF THE KING

We come now to the second part of our task—the work to be done by the children themselves. First Communion is the great epoch in a child's life, having its influence on the whole career. It is the time when its conscience is trained, its will braced, its principles of action formed. If we take so much pains to fix the attention and arouse interest, it is that we may ensure lasting results in the life and conduct.

Let us be definite here, and practical. We must show the children that the chief part of preparation must be their own doing. It does not consist merely in coming to instructions and learning their catechism, but in setting earnestly to work to correct the faults which they know our Lord will not like to find in their hearts when He comes.

Put before them now in very simple language the Child Life of Him who—a child like themselves—is coming to them to help them to be like Him. Show Him to them in His home life, at His prayer, at His play, at His lessons, in His troubles; and tell them they will best please Him and make ready for His coming by trying to be like Him.

Teach them how to meet temptation; to rise promptly and without discouragement after a fall; to offer their daily actions to God, and to turn to Him at once in time of trouble. Teach them the necessity of prayer, and of perseverance in it to the end. Familiarise them with the thought of the Presence of God as a safeguard in temptation and a help in every need. These things are not spiritual luxuries for the favoured few. We all need them to keep out of sin and to store our lives with the merit that lies in our daily path.

And now is our chance with the children. Never again shall we have a right to claim them so entirely for a course of instruction. Never again will their hearts be so fresh, so teachable, so eager. Oh, let us do all we can for them *now!* Let us impress upon them the duty of morning and night prayer and examination of conscience, of attendance at Sunday Mass, of regular approach to the Sacraments, of observance of the Church's law of abstinence. In a word, let us get them to look upon fidelity to the practices of a Christian life as the real preparation our Lord asks of them, and to expect from His Presence with them great strength and help in the battle with self for which each one of them must be prepared. All this cannot be done before First Communion, but it can be *begun*, and taken up afterwards, as the best means of profiting by the grace they have received and of disposing themselves for what our Lord has in store for them in His further visits.

It is all-important, then, that the child, young as it is, should take itself in hand at this time, that our instructions should tend, not only to inform its mind as to certain dogmas, but to stimulate its will. We must get it to take an interest in its own soul, to see that it ought to do something itself to get ready for Jesus. The work of preparation, we may hope, has not to be *begun* now. "That most serious and critical event in the Christian's life, the First Communion, which the child receives as it steps forth into the battle"[1] should find the little hands

1   Pastoral Letter for Lent, 1893. Bishop Hedley.

already trained to war. Gradually, under the mother's watchful eye, it should have been formed to habits of reverence for God and holy things, of obedience, self-restraint, truthfulness, consideration for others. But how often, alas! has its lot been the reverse of this. How often has home fostered the seeds of evil and done a work which it must be the labour of life to undo.

In any case, and under whatever influences a child has come, our task now will be the same—to teach it in simple words its duty to God, to others, and to itself; to teach it to fear sin, to overcome temptation, to give up its own will, to offer its actions and its troubles to God—in a word, to set about the sanctification of daily life, which can never be begun too soon. Little children are generous, and readily make efforts for anything that appeals to them. They will be prompt in rising, faithful to morning and night prayers and examination of conscience, obedient to parents, unselfish to companions, to please Jesus and get ready for Him. Thus good habits may be formed. Never again shall we have so powerful a motive to put before them. Surely we ought to utilise it, with prudence certainly, but also with zeal.

It would be well that such practical instruction should be given, not after we have gone through the Life of our Lord with the children, but along with it. By this means we shall be able at the outset to put something definite before them as their preparation for His coming, and to fall back continually on the lessons of His Life for the example and encouragement they need.

And here again let us remind ourselves that our words will be persuasive in proportion to the earnestness of our own practice. Without enthusiasm no great and lasting work is done by a teacher. And enthusiasm cannot be counterfeited. It must be the product of our own intense conviction and experience.

Hence, were it only in the interest of our little charges, we shall review our own observance. Our Lord's marvellous words, "For them do I sanctify Myself," will appeal to us now with special force, and our own spiritual life will be quickened by our zeal for the little ones entrusted to us.

A story is a good start always. To impress upon the minds of the children the importance of the great act for which they are going to prepare, we may tell them Napoleon's answer when at the height of his glory he was questioned as to the happiest day of his life.[1] Or give the conversation that took place years later between the fallen Emperor and the little girl he came across in his island-prison of St. Helena:—

"How old are you, my child?"

"Twelve years old, Sire."

"You have made your First Communion?"

"No, Sire, there is no one here to instruct me."

"Then I will do so myself."

From that day master and pupil were seen together every morning, seated on a bench in earnest conversation. Might not the distant guards, as they watched their august prisoner at his task, have felt that the words to his brilliant court at Versailles had not been idly spoken!

Or we may awaken the children's interest and enlist the service of the imagination in the work we are about, by means of an allegory.

Say you are going to tell them a story—not a common story, not a fairytale, though it sounds like one, but a story called a parable. Parables have two meanings, one that any baby can see, and a secret one—one that has to be found out by thinking. They must find out the secret meaning of your story as you go along. You once told it to some children who were as still

1   He replied: " The day of my first communion was the happiest day of my life, for then I was brought nearest to my God."

as mice all the time you were talking, trying who could find out most. There they sat, counting on their fingers what they found out. And—only think!—in the end they had found out more things than you had. You did feel proud of that class; it is so nice to teach children who are bright and sharp like that. By the look of the faces you see now, you think you will have to be proud of some other children.

Well! are all ready and the fingers ready—you are going to begin:—

There was once a King so good and kind, that all good people loved him. He lived in a bright, sunny land, where his happy subjects, called courtiers, lived with him. There was no hunger, no cold, no unkindness, no pain or trouble of any kind in that land. But the King had another land far away. There it was cold and dull, and the people were poor and full of troubles. The greatest trouble was this. A certain bad lord, very strong and cruel, used to go about, killing or hurting all the people he could catch, even the little children who had never done him any harm. I will tell you why.

He had once been a servant of the King, and the King had been very kind to him, and made him grand and rich. But this wicked servant instead of thanking the King and loving him, turned against him, and tried to make all the good servants bad like himself. Of course he was punished. He was turned out of the bright land, and all the beautiful things the King had given him were taken from him. This made him very angry and spiteful. He could not hurt the King, but he went into the far-off land where the King's poor people lived, to try and make them bad, that they might be punished and unhappy as he was. Day and night he went amongst them, trying to kill them, or hurt them, or frighten them, and all because they were the King's people and going some day to be with the King in the happy land, where he had once been.

Now the King heard all this and it made him very sad, for he loved his poor people and could not bear to think of their pain. He thought what he could do to help them, and at last he said: "I know what I will do. I will go to them myself, and then I shall be able to help them better. The cruel lord is afraid of me, because he knows I am stronger than he is. I will go into my people's little houses and then he will not dare to come in."

So word was sent to say the King was coming.

At once there was a stir all through the land. Everybody began to get ready. The messengers said that though the King was very kind, there were two things he could not bear—dirt and disorder. All who wanted to please him and get the presents he was bringing, must get their houses clean and tidy.

I said everybody *began* to get ready. But—sad to say—some only began. They soon got tired and left off. They saw their neighbours working hard, children working hard, getting rid of ugly things, mending, polishing, buying or borrowing whatever would make the little cottages look pretty. They were told that those who tried most would get most, that no one could get the houses ready but the owners. They heard all this—and did nothing, or very little. What happened? The long-expected Day came at last. They did just what they were obliged to do, but they could not all in a minute make their cottages like the bright little homes all round.

It would have done you good to see the King's face when he saw all that his people had done—when he read: "Welcome!" and "Long live the King!" on every side. He had to stoop to get into the little houses, the doors were so low. All his grand train who had come with him stayed outside, for beside the rooms being very small, the King did not want any one there but the owner and himself. There was important business to be done, and he had secrets for each. Floor, ceiling, whitewashed walls—how poor it all was, how different from what he was used to! Yet his face showed real pleasure as he looked round, and saw all that had been going on for months to get ready for him. There was a smile on his lips, and he even said he was delighted to be with those who had made him so welcome.

Then came the presents. Opening his treasures, he took out his gifts and set them before the delighted eyes of the poor folk—presents so costly, that even the King had had to buy them at the price of his own blood. And—better still—the gifts were not costly only, but useful, exactly what was wanted by each. The King must surely have known all about every one of them, to choose his gifts so wisely.

What a happy time they had together, the King and his poor servants! For he was so gentle and kind that they were not afraid to tell him all their troubles, and to ask his advice and help. Yet not all were so glad and happy. From some of the houses the King came out when the visit was over, carrying most of the presents he had meant to leave. There was nowhere to set them down. The place was so dusty, not to say dirty, that his beautiful gifts would have been out of place. And then he was not asked for anything. The people all knew his rule, "Ask, and you shall receive." But these lazy ones did not take the trouble to ask. And so, though he did give them things, they were nothing like so well off as the others.

You would have been pleased to see the little houses all bright with the gifts of the King. And the owners were bright too. They might well be. For the King had told them many secrets, and comforted them wonderfully. He had shown them the tricks of the cruel lord who lived near and how to be a match for him. He had promised to help them whenever they asked him for help. And—oh, was not this kind!—he said he would come and see them as often as they liked, and give them whatever they asked for that would be good for them to have. In short, he left them so cheered up that you would not have known them to be the poor, sad creatures of a while ago.

"Now, how many have found out what this story means? Let us begin at the beginning and see what we can make out? The kind King—who is He? And His happy courtiers who live with Him? And His poor people far away? The Great Day of the Royal Visit—who knows what all these mean?"

You may perhaps find it advisable to give the children a clue almost at the start. Watch the faces and the fingers as you go along, and help them to any extent if they cannot see the meaning, and interest flags. If they have been interested in the story—and they should he if you have told it with animation and plenty of gesture; *told it*, mind, in your own words, not *read it*—you may find it useful to refer to from time to time. Anything that fixes the imagination and deals with the concrete, is a help in dealing with little ones.

The application, of course, is what matters. The rest is useful only as the needle for drawing the thread. "Who is the Great King who is coming to them? Hands up—those who are going to get ready for Him. Are there going to be any lazy ones?" (look round). "No. Well, that is all right. We are all going to begin, and we will try not to get tired and leave off. What is it our dear Lord will not like to find in our souls? What kind of sin would drive Him away altogether? What smaller sins would not drive Him away, but be disagreeable to Him? Let us think if we have any of these ugly things in our hearts. If we have, let us begin to get rid of them now, and pick out one or two of the worst that we will turn out before He comes. We shall not do this all at once. The people we have been thinking about could not do all at once. But little by little they got ready. This ugly thing was got out of the way, this good thing was mended, that was polished up. And at last all began to look tidy, bright, and pleasant. So will it be with us. The bad habit of looking all about at prayers will have to be changed. The good resolution we have made to get up quickly in the morning, and to do as we are told at once, has got broken. We must make up our minds again to do these things, and then it will be mended. Perhaps the good habit of examination of conscience at night has grown rusty, and wants polishing up. We must look into our hearts and see what is wanted. When we find at our night prayers that we have done something naughty that day, we will tell Jesus we are sorry, and that we will try not to do it another day. This is getting our souls ready for Him."

Among the lessons we may teach from our Lord's life, the chief will be reverence at prayer, obedience to parents and teachers, kindness to others. We shall have done much if we have laid the foundation of these three things. Another practice, in which even tiny children can show themselves wonderfully generous, is the making of little sacrifices and the gaining of little victories over themselves.

We might propose one or more points to them as their own part in the preparation, what *they are going to do themselves* to get the little houses ready for the King. Sometimes a card given to them as a reminder or a record helps.

FOR OUR DEAR LORD on MY FIRST COMMUNION DAY (*Date*)	
Good Morning and Night Prayers	
Good Lessons at School and Home	
Obeying Quickly and Helping Mother	
Things done to please Jesus	

They put a prick for each act, and keep the cards privately and carefully as a present to our Lord on their First Communion Day. It is quite conceivable that the discussion, comparison, and pricking of cards might become a serious difficulty in a teacher's way during school hours and prove a positive nuisance. This could be prevented by saying the cards were to be kept at home, and the pricking done at the examination of conscience in their night prayers—a device that would make this irksome duty attractive! But cards are merely a suggestion, which can be taken for what it is worth. As a reminder of something definite to aim at, they are eagerly accepted by children, and often used with a generosity and perseverance that might put some of their elders to shame. We expect children "to be better" during this time of preparation, and perhaps our ideas of betterness are of the vaguest. This is unfair to them. They want to be *doing something*, and it is our business to see that so valuable a disposition and opportunity are not thrown away. If cards are impracticable, we must cast about for some other way of obtaining *definite results* in the improvement of daily conduct.

Tell the children to try not to do little sins (give examples); to drive away temptation at once, saying, "Jesus, Mary, help me," or some other short prayer. Tell them to try to say their prayers well, remembering before they begin that God is there, seeing them and loving them; to be obedient to their parents and teachers, useful at home, and kind to their companions; to be honest, truthful, forgiving. Do not be afraid to repeat the same thing again and again. Children do not weary of repetition as we do, and it is the only way of making the desired impression. But they do weary of anything lengthy, and of what they cannot understand—who shall blame them!

A Sister of Charity of much experience strongly recommends as an excellent resolution to put before even little children, that of making themselves useful at home—"helping mother." It checks the tendency to idleness, selfishness, and independence so prevalent in our days, cultivates an intelligent interest in the details of home life, which is simply invaluable, and, above all, draws mother and child together by a sympathy which will be the safeguard, strength, and happiness of both.

We might give instructions on the subjects named on the card, going into details, and drawing the children out by questions which keep up interest and afford such a valuable index to the workings of their minds. For example, "How could they be useful to mother?" "What little victory could they gain over themselves to please Jesus?" If cards are used, we may now and again express the hope that they are doing well, but it is better for obvious reasons not to express a wish to see them. In short, we should show a constant, loving interest in the children's efforts, and do all we can to keep up the spirit of joyous anticipation of the Great Day.

As a stimulus in another direction, the Synod of Westminster suggests marks: "Catechists should keep a book, into which they should enter the marks deserved by each child for conduct and proficiency. These marks are: V.G., *Very Good*; G., *Good*; F.G., *Fairly Good*; V.F., *Very Fair*; P., *Passed*; F., *Failure*. Once a month the Catechist should read out the marks gained by each child, and should try by words of encouragement to excite interest and emulation among the children."

VII
LEARN OF ME

It is not safe, surely, to trust to the Morning Prayers said at school for the foundation of a habit which is to last through life. Unless children are taught to say their prayers before they leave their room—for this two minutes will suffice—there is danger of these being omitted altogether when school life is over.

Teach them, then, on waking, to give their first thoughts to God by saying some short prayer, such as: "O my God, I give Thee my heart and my soul"; to rise quickly at the proper time, and as soon as they are dressed to kneel down and say their morning prayers. Teach them some form which will include the *Our Father, Hail Mary, I believe*, short Acts of Faith, Hope, and Charity, an offering to God of their daily actions and troubles, the intention of gaining all the Indulgences they can, and a commendation of themselves to our Lady, their Angel Guardian, and Patron Saints.

A FORM OF MORNING PRAYERS

✠ In the Name of the Father, and of the Son, and of the Holy Ghost. Amen.

Our Father. Hail Mary. I believe.

My God, I believe in Thee, because Thou art truth itself.

My God, I hope in Thee, because of Thy promises to me.

My God, I love Thee, because Thou art so good; teach me to love Thee daily more and more and to love everybody for Thy sake.

My God, because Thou art so good, I am sorry for all my sins; help me not to sin again.

> "My God, I offer Thee this day
> All I shall think, or do, or say,
> Uniting it with what was done
> On earth by Jesus Christ, Thy Son."

I wish to gain all the Indulgences[1] I can.

Holy Mary, be a mother to me.

My Good Angel, take care of me.

My Patron Saints, pray for me.

My God, keep me from sin to-day; make me a good child always, and take me to Heaven when I die.

Bless my Father, mother, brothers, and sisters, and all for whom I ought to pray.

May our Lord ✠ bless us and keep us from all evil, and bring us to life everlasting. May the souls of the faithful departed, through the mercy of God, rest in peace. Amen.

A FORM OF NIGHT PRAYERS[2]

✠ In the Name of the Father, and of the Son, and of the Holy Ghost. Amen.

---

1 Tell the children Indulgence means letting people off punishment. Indulgenced prayers let us off some of the punishment of our sins which we must bear here or in Purgatory. After we have been to Communion we can gain more Indulgences than before.

2 These, too, should be short and said at a fixed time. Oh, that we could see restored the custom of family prayer at night! Is it reasonable to hold our little ones responsible for their prayers, morning and evening? Yet how few mothers think of their own responsibility in this respect. As things are, all we can do to secure night prayers being said, is to make them as short as possible, and to train the children to kneel down and say them before they go to bed.

Our Father. Hail Mary. I confess.

My God, I believe that Thou art here, that Thou dost see me, and hear me, and love me. I thank Thee for taking care of me to-day. Help me to see what sins I have done and to be sorry for them.

(*Here wait a little, and think:*
- Have I thought, or said, or done anything to-day that I know was wrong?
- Have I said my prayers carelessly in church, in school, or at home?
- Have I been disobedient to my parents or teachers?
- Have I been unkind to my companions?
- Have I been untruthful, angry, greedy, lazy, naughty in any way?

Then say :)

My God, I am very sorry that I have offended Thee. I love Thee with all my heart because Thou art so good, and I will not sin again.

Lord Jesus, receive my soul.

Holy Mary, be a mother to me.

My Good Angel, watch over me this night.

My Patron Saints, pray for me.

O my God, bless my father, mother, brothers, and sisters, and all for whom I ought to pray.

May our Lord ✠ bless us, and keep us from all evil, and bring us to life everlasting. May the souls of the faithful departed, through the mercy of God, rest in peace. Amen.

It is a good practice to kneel down and make an act of contrition just before we get into bed. We might die in the night.

Set the Child Jesus before the children as an example of reverence at prayer, of kindness and obedience. Show Him to them kneeling beside His Mother, saying His morning and night prayers, His eyes cast down, His little hands joined. He did not look about, nor turn His head when the door opened, nor think about His play. He knew He was speaking to God and He knelt there reverent, and still, thinking of what He was saying. When His prayers were said, He went out to play.

And how kind He was then. Every one wanted to play with Him, to be on His side in the games. He did not try to be first always, or to have all the best things for Himself. He had very few nice things because He was a poor Child, and His Mother had only poor things to give Him. But what He had He shared with His little companions. He tried to please them. So they all loved Him, and used to tell Him their troubles, and let Him make up their quarrels. They used to call Him "Little Sweetness,"[1] and when they were in trouble they would say, "Let us go and tell Little Sweetness all about it; He will comfort us." They knew He was always fair; He always told the truth; He was always kind.

And they saw how obedient He was. When His Mother stood at the door of the little cottage and called Him, He did not complain or ask to stay longer. But He left His play, and went in at once, and did quite cheerfully what He had to do next, even if He did not like to do it.

Why? Because He wanted His little First Communicants to be like Him, and so He showed them how to do all these things. Who can tell, now, some of the things in which we can try to be like Him?

The Sacred Infancy is a whole storehouse of lessons from which we can draw later on when we are less pressed. Take, for instance, the Flight into Egypt.

Tell the story. How, "when little Jesus was quite a baby, cruel King Herod wanted to kill Him lest He should take his

1   St. Bonaventure.

crown from him when He grew up. So he told the wise men who had seen the star in the East to go to Bethlehem, and when they had found the Child to come back and tell him, that he, too, might go and adore Him. They did not know how wicked the king was; they could not see what he was thinking in his mind. But God saw, and took care of the holy Child. He told the wise men not to return to Herod, but to go back another way into their own country. Then He sent an Angel to St. Joseph by night to tell him to get up and take little Jesus and His Mother and go into a country called Egypt where they would be safe. St. Joseph got up at once and went out and saddled the ass for Mary to ride on. And she woke her little Babe and wrapped Him in such poor clothes as she had, to keep Him from the cold, and then the three went out into the dark night. They had to go on for many days and nights. The days were hot with the burning sun, the nights were chill with the desert winds and dews. But they were quite cheerful, because they were doing what God told them, and Jesus was with them. They were not afraid either, though they knew wild beasts were about, and cruel men were looking for the holy Child and would kill Him if they could find Him.

"When Herod found the wise men did not come back, he was very angry and sent his soldiers to Bethlehem to kill the Child. But He was gone, and no one knew where. Then Herod was more angry still and told the soldiers to kill all the babies they could find. The poor mothers cried bitterly, and the babies cried; but it was no use, wherever they were found they were killed."

Some one is sure to ask why God let them be killed, and why He did not kill wicked King Herod instead. Say "we do not always know why God lets people do bad things. But we know He is always wise and good, and if He lets good people have troubles, and be poor, or sick, or sad, it is because He wants to give them a great prize some day for bearing these things bravely. So it is often His best friends whom He lets suffer most, because He wants to give them the best prizes. He loved His dear Mother more than any one in the world. Yet He let her suffer more than any one else, because she was to be Queen of Heaven and have the brightest crown there.

"If we have to bear a little pain here, and bear it bravely to please God, He will give us everything we want in Heaven. There is no pain there, but all the people are happy, and glad of the pain they bore bravely in this world. The poor babies did not like being killed by the soldiers. But when they got into Heaven and found what a nice place it is, they were glad they had come so soon. Perhaps if they had lived to be grown up, they would have been wicked men and never got to Heaven at all. God always loves us and takes care of us. If He lets pain or trouble come to us, He never lets it be too hard. And when the trouble is over, He will give us a great reward which will last for ever."

You can ask the children:—

"Who is it that lets trouble come to us?

"Why does He let it come?

"Does it show He does not love us?

"Why did He let His dear Mother suffer so much?

"What must we do when we are in pain or trouble?

"May we ask God to take the pain away?

"But if it does not go—what then?

"Shall we learn a little prayer to say when we are in trouble? 'My God, Thy Will be done,' 'Dear Jesus, help me.' "

In this way we may teach many useful lessons. Make them all practical. Bring them to bear upon the children's daily life and small experiences. At the same time we must beware of piling lessons or even stories one upon another. One worked out in detail will make more impression than two; as a rule, the second only serves to drive out the first.

We come now to the immediate preparation for First Communion.

VII
IMMEDIATE PREPARATION

See that the children understand that to make a good Communion the soul must he free from mortal sin, and the body must be fasting from twelve o'clock the night before.

Preparation of the Soul.—If any one had committed a mortal sin, he could not go to Holy Communion till he had been to confession. It would not be enough to make an act of contrition. We might go to Communion if we had committed venial sins, but we should try not to do anything that would displease our dear Lord who is coming to us and who loves us so dearly. If we have been greedy, or careless at our prayers, or unkind, we should make an act of contrition directly: "My God, I am very sorry for having done this, because You are so good; help me not to do it again."

But we should not only try to get rid of sin, but to make our souls pleasing to our Lord by being good, and by often asking Him to come and stay with us. We may ask His Blessed Mother to give us the Infant Jesus to hold in our arms for a little while.

Let us say to her:—

"Mother sweet and Mother fair,
    Give me Jesus now to hold;
I will take the greatest care,
    I will keep Him from the cold,
I will love Him tenderly,—
    Please, oh! please, do give Him me."

Let them learn well the verses which follow that they may know what to say to our Lord when He comes. Tell them they may say the verses before Communion anywhere and as often as they like—in church, in the street, at home, if they lie awake at night. Our Lord wants to come to them very much and is counting the days. He likes us to count them too.

Preparation of the Body.—Out of respect for the Body of our Lord, we may not take anything in the way of food, drink, or even medicine after twelve o'clock, the night before our Communion. If, without thinking, we were to take something, we must not go to Communion that day. There was no harm and no one will scold us, we can go another day, but it would be a great sin to go on a day when we had broken our fast.

Let us take care that our dealings with these little ones are such that they would not be afraid to tell us in such a case. Let them feel we should be sorry for them and not scold them. Much harm might happen otherwise. See that they know the kind of things that do not break the fast—dust, hair, a drop of rain, what was in the mouth before twelve. Tell them not to be frightened about the fast, because unless they know they have eaten or drunk something, they are right in thinking they have not, and can go to Communion.

They should also be clean and tidy, but must not mind if their clothes are poor. Our Lord does not mind. He loves the poor. He does not care for pretty things. He looks at our hearts not at our clothes, and will give us a double welcome if we are poor.

IX
THE FIRST COMMUNION DAY

See that the children are in church in good time. They may say, or perhaps sing, the following verses which they will know by heart.

I. BEFORE COMMUNION

Think you are in the Cave of Bethlehem, and that you ask our Blessed Lady to give you the Infant Jesus to hold in your arms for a little while. Say to her—

> "Mother Mary, Mother dear,
>   Lend thy little Babe to me;
> I believe that He is here
>   Just the same as on thy knee;
> I want to kiss His little Feet,—
>   Give me Jesus, Mother sweet.

> "I will clasp Him safe and warm,
>   Mother dear, against my breast,
> And no sin shall do Him harm,
>   And I will always love Him best.
> I will hold Him tenderly,—
>   Give Him, Mother dear, to me.

"Mother sweet and Mother fair,
  Give me Jesus now to hold;
I will take the greatest care,
  I will keep Him from the cold,
I will love Him tenderly,—
  Please, oh! please, do give Him me."

They may say all together after you the intentions for which they offer their Communion:—

"Dear Jesus,...I am coming to You...because You want me to come...and because I love You...I thank You...because You are so good and kind to me...because You have borne... so much pain for me...I am very sorry...for all I have ever done...to make You sad...I am sure You will give me...what I ask for to-day...Please bless...our holy Father the Pope,...my father and mother,...brothers and sisters...and all I ought to pray for...Help all the people...who do not love You...to be sorry...and to love You...Help the poor Souls in Purgatory... Help me...to be a good child...after my First Communion... Help me to be good always...and take me to Heaven...when I die.

"Dear Mother Mary,...pray to Jesus for me.

"My dear Angel Guardian,...pray for me...and take me to Jesus.

ADORATION AND FAITH

"Jesus! Thou art coming
  Holy as Thou art,
Thou the God who made me,
  To my little heart.

Jesus, I believe it
  On Thy only word;
Kneeling, I adore thee
  As my King and Lord.

HUMILITY AND SORROW

Who am I, my Jesus,
   That Thou com'st to me?
I have sinned against Thee
   Often, cruelly.

I am very sorry
   I have caused Thee pain,
I will never, never
   Wound Thy heart again.

TRUST

Put Thy kind arms round me.
   Feeble as I am:
Thou art my Good Shepherd,
   I Thy little lamb.
Since Thou comest, Jesus,
   Now to be my guest,
I can trust Thee always,
   Lord, for all the rest.

LOVE AND DESIRE

Dearest Lord, I love Thee,
   With my whole, whole heart:
Not for what Thou givest,
   But for what Thou art.
Come, oh, come sweet Saviour,
   Come to me, and stay,
For I want Thee, Jesus,
   More than I can say.

OFFERING AND PETITION

Ah! what gift or present,
   Jesus, can I bring?
I have nothing worthy
   Of my God and King;
But thou art my Shepherd,
   I Thy little lamb;
Take myself, dear Jesus,
   All I have and am.

> Take my body, Jesus,
>> Eyes, and ears, and tongue;
> Never let them, Jesus,
>> Help to do Thee wrong.
> Take my heart and fill it
>> Full of love for Thee,
> All I have I give Thee,
>> Give Thyself to me."

The children will have been taught how to go up to the rails— hands joined, without gloves, eyes cast down; to hold the cloth like a little table under the chin; to keep the eyes closed, the head straight up, the tongue put out so as to cover the lower lip entirely. After receiving, to draw in the tongue gently, close the mouth, let the Sacred Host moisten a little, and swallow it as soon as they can. Should it stick to the roof of the mouth, to remove it with the tongue. Tell them we may never touch the Blessed Sacrament with our finger.

When the priest lays the Sacred Host on your tongue, think that our Blessed Lady lays the infant Jesus gently in your arms. Carry Him carefully back to your place, whispering to Him—

> "Baby Jesus, wilt Thou lie
>> In my arms a little while?
> I will hold Thee tenderly,
>> Look at Thee, and Thou wilt smile.
> Jesus, Jesus, God and Man,
>> I will love Thee all I can."

When back in your place after Communion think you go into a corner of the Cave at Bethlehem, and there kneel down, holding the Divine Babe quite close against your heart. Say to Him—

> "O Jesus dear, O Jesus dear,
>> I am so glad to hold Thee here!
> Although Thou art so weak and small,
>> Thou art my God, and Lord of all.
>
> O Babe divine, O Babe divine,
>> Just for a little Thou art mine,
> And I can press Thee to my heart,
>> All great and holy as Thou art.

My Brother sweet, my Brother sweet,
I kiss Thy tender little feet,
And lay my face against Thy cheek,
And am too happy quite to speak.

Dear Infant Jesus, do not cry,
For I will really, really try
Never to hurt Thee any more,
Never to make thy sweet heart sore.

O Jesus dear, O Jesus dear,
I want to have Thee always near,
I want my little heart to be
A soft, white cradle-bed for Thee."

Then they may speak to our Lord in any little prayers they know. As few, perhaps, will have books or know how to read easily, it will be well to have taught them short aspirations which they know so well as to remember them almost without effort:

"Jesus, my God, I love Thee above all things."

"O Sacrament most holy, O Sacrament Divine,
All praise and all thanksgiving be every moment Thine."

"Sweet Sacrament, we thee adore,
Oh! make us love Thee more and more."

You might help them in their thanksgiving by some short prayers said after you:

"Dear Jesus...remember You said:...'Ask and you shall receive'... I am going to ask You now...for what I want...I want to love You very much...I want to show You that I love You...by not doing any sins...even little ones...and by trying... to please You...by all I do...by my prayers...by my lessons...by my play...I want to do all these things...to please You...Help me, dear Lord...because I cannot be good by myself...Help me to say my prayers well...to be obedient...to be kind...to be patient...when I am in pain or trouble...to say 'No' quickly... when the devil wants me to do what is wrong...Help me to remember...that You can see me always...in the streets...in my bed at night...when I am playing with others...when I am quite by myself...Never let me do anything...that would make You angry with me...Never in my whole life...let me do a mortal sin...I will try not to be naughty...but if I am sometimes...help me to be sorry directly...to say: 'My God I am sorry'... and then to try again...

Dear Lord, I give You my heart...Keep it for Yourself...I give it to You...for Your very own...I give You...my body and my soul...all I think and do and say...till I come to You again... Keep me always...a good Catholic...and take me to Heaven... when I die...Take care of all I love...of all I ought to pray for... of our Holy Father the Pope...and of Thy Holy Church...of our country...of our schools...Have pity on all poor sinners...and save them from hell...and take the poor Souls in Purgatory... out of their pain."

Say: "We are going to say the prayer before the crucifix now for these poor Souls:

'Behold, O kind,' &c.

Then we say five times Our Father and Hail Mary for the Pope's intentions that God will make all people good Catholics, that they may be kind to one another, and not go to war."

Do what you can to make the First Communion day bright and happy, as bright and happy as possible. If there is a procession and Benediction in the evening, gather the First Communicants together in the church for our Lord's Blessing. Teach them to thank Him for His visit by thinking of Him sometimes during the day and saying some little prayer, such as, "Dear Jesus, I love You, I thank You." or "Dear Jesus, come again," or one of the verses they said in the morning when our Lord was with them—trying too to please Him in what they do. This is the way to make Him want to come again.

X
AFTER FIRST COMMUNION

Now comes the call for solicitude and zeal on the part of the teacher. Now is the time for seeking that co-operation of mothers (see "Home Influence") which will help to preserve the fruits of our Lord's Presence in the hearts of our little ones. We must remind ourselves, and keep reminding ourselves, how very little they are. They have come up to the altar-rails at the bidding of the Church, and have received into their souls more grace than we can dream of. But the vessels are small and frail. Our help is needed to strengthen them that they may not only keep what they have, but increase their treasure in every fresh reception. If only we can get the aid of mothers now, how much may be done. *They* must see that the Communions are regularly made. And *we* must devise means for keeping up the children's desire for the Heavenly Bread they have tasted.

It has been said that a personal love of our Lord is the only force that will carry us safely through the dangers and trials of life to the end of our journey. The foundation for such a love ought to have been laid in the First Communion instructions. His own blessed Presence after Communion will, we may hope, keep it alive. But here as everywhere He looks for our concurrence. Devotion to the Sacred Heart is nothing else but the personal love of Christ, and the Apostleship of Prayer is its natural expression.

Little children of seven are quite able to understand the main features of the Apostleship. How we want to love our dear Lord as His friends on earth—His Blessed Mother, St. Joseph, St. Mary Magdalen, St. John loved Him. How we must show our love as they did—more by acts than by words. How we must be glad to help Him, glad to work for Him, to suffer for Him, as the Apostles were. The youngest of us can be an Apostle by doing what the Apostles did—helping to save souls for Jesus by their work, their good example, their sufferings, and above all by their prayers. Those who want to help our Lord can do so in all these ways, especially by prayer. Their Apostleship is called the Apostleship of Prayer. The prayer of little children is very powerful. God loves to hear it. When the Jews were in trouble, they used to fetch a number of Jewish babies and put them down before the Tabernacle to pray. Much more can little Christian children before our Tabernacles get great things from God.

They can be taught what is meant by our Lord's intentions, and how by saying the prayer: "Thy Kingdom come," we help Him to get what His Sacred Heart desires. Those who belong to the Apostleship of Prayer can gain an indulgence whenever they say that short prayer.

In the morning offering of the Apostleship of Prayer we offer our Lord—that means give Him for His own—all the prayer, work, and sufferings of that day, to help Him to save the souls He loves. This offering puts a holy mark on all these things, and will get us a great reward in Heaven. And it makes us share in all the good works of the thousands and thousands of people who belong to the Apostleship. If we forget to make it there is no harm, only we shall not share that day in the good done by the other members of the Apostleship, just as a person going to a picnic and bringing nothing for the company, could hardly expect to share in all the good things brought by the others.

These few points, simplified and well illustrated, will make the children eager to belong to the Apostleship. And we could hardly do our Lord a more acceptable service, or take better means to keep up, not Communions only, but fervent Communions, than to present Him with this troop of infant Apostles. But the enrolment must be more than a mere ceremony. It must express the children's desire to do something for our Lord—a desire we shall take care to foster by interesting them gradually in works of zeal, and teaching them now to value the prayer, work, and suffering which can do so much for God and for souls.

XI
HOME INFLUENCE

Experience shows us that, next to the grace of God, those who have the welfare of First Communicants at heart must look to the mothers. Pains may be taken by others to reach the child's intelligence, heart, and will, but they will be rendered to a great extent ineffectual if the home influence does not tell in the same direction. It has been found that much may be done towards securing the co-operation of mothers if, on the formation of a First Communion class, they can have their responsibilities and power for good brought home to them in a familiar talk.

Get them to see that preparation for First Communion is not simply a time for informing the child's mind by teaching it a certain number of facts respecting the Blessed Sacrament. It is the preparation of the young heart for our Lord's coming by the exercise of those Christian virtues and the formation of those Christian habits which must be its stay through life. For this the proper sphere is the home. Routine may influence it in the school. There it goes with the crowd. It is at home that individual effort is called out and that good habits are formed. "In the school and from the lips of the priest," says one of our Bishops, "the instruction is given in due time. But before the mystery of the Eucharist can become a living and real conception to the mind, there must be a gradual progress in piety, reverence, and refinement of thought...The Catholic child should learn day by day to join its hands together and pray with childlike faith to its Father Who is in Heaven. It should never hear God's most Holy Name uttered except with reverential awe. It should become familiar with pious pictures and images, which will leave their impression upon its young imagination. It should hear of the Saints and of the Holy Mother of God. It should be accustomed to the solemnity of the Church, where the altar is, and should learn to watch, and by degrees to understand, what is done when the Priest of God, in his robes of priesthood, stands in silence before that altar and utters the words which send him on the instant to his knees. These things the child hears of in the school, but if it hears them only there, it will with difficulty take in the idea of the Blessed Sacrament. Moreover, during all that time of opening and expanding intelligence, it should be gradually accustomed to self-restraint, to purity, to refinement in word and deed, and to a horror of sin in every form. Not only is the idea of the Blessed Sacrament difficult to implant in a child who is positively wicked, but the same is true of one who is uncared for, neglected, dirty, and left chiefly on the streets. It is evident that this must be so; for the young minds and hearts of such unfortunate children are harassed, sullied, and preoccupied, and the thought of Jesus and His mysterious love must be as strange to them as to the savage. Where there should be a pious love of God there is a premature worldliness; where there should be innocence, there is a precocious knowledge of all that is evil; and where there should be the gentleness and self-respect of one who possesses an immortal soul made to God's own image there is too often a coarseness and selfishness, a hardness and recklessness which would be disgusting even in grown men and women. To prepare children of this kind for their

First Communion as the pastor's heart would wish to prepare them, is impossible. Sufficient knowledge may be imparted to them, it is true, and by great exertions they may be brought to the Sacrament of Penance and kept in some degree of decent behaviour for a day or two until the sacred ceremony is over... But it is too probable that, for want of the preparation here spoken of, the marvellous graces which the Blessed Eucharist is intended to bring to the soul of the Christian will never be 'stirred up.' They will lie latent and useless in the soul for want of that piety and that sense of God and of holy things which, as a rule, are not imparted by grace without the co-operation of pastors, teachers, and surroundings. For grace does not work miracles; at least, we have no right to expect that it will; and whenever human and natural agency has its sphere of work, such agency must be given...It should be clearly understood, in the first place, that the First Communion of a child is a matter which concerns not only the priest but the parent...All the zeal of the pastor is marred unless the parents also do their part. They are bound, at least, to do two things. First, they must see that the children attend the special instructions which are given to the First Communicants. Is it not very hard upon the priest, and a proof of great indifference to Almighty God, when children are allowed by their parents persistently to stay away from and to neglect that very instruction which is especially intended to make them less unworthy and less unprepared for this, one of the greatest events of their lives? In the name of God, let parents, and especially mothers, do their best to prevent this grievous misfortune. When they find out, either from its being announced in church or in any other way, that any child of theirs is to begin preparation for First Communion, let them take careful note of it, and let them at once make the boy or girl understand that they at least—the parents—are aware how great and important an event is coming on. Let them redouble their vigilance and their solicitude, and by firmness and kindness ensure that there shall be no neglect; otherwise, if the child misses its Communion the guilt will be upon their souls. And how many do this? How many young men, especially, are found every year who have never made their First Communion? We may be very sure it was in great part the fault of their parents.

In the second place comes the wider and more difficult duty of training up the child in piety and spiritual feeling, so that when our Lord comes He may come to a heart that is truly able to give Him a welcome and an abiding dwelling-place. To speak practically on this matter it is necessary to insist that parents keep their young children off the streets and away from evil companions. This can only be done, as regards poor people, by taking a great deal more trouble than mothers generally take. But it is a trouble which, if they do not take, they will incur the anger and condemnation of God. They must take the trouble first to give good example themselves, and, secondly, to watch over their children. Children cannot be kept always in the house, and they must be allowed to amuse themselves; and, moreover, the mother is too often hard worked herself. But it is absolutely necessary, if we would save our young people from that vice and degradation which begins in childhood with roughness, dirt, and recklessness, to have the children watched. Some means must be found out of doing it: an elder sister or a neighbour may help; or the children may be entrusted to good companions; or sometimes they may be kept by the mother's side. But somehow or other it must be done; because parents who cannot maintain a reasonable watch over their young families have no business to have families at all.

Let us be persuaded that on the Blessed Sacrament depends our eternal salvation, and on the First Communion depends, in very great measure, all the Communions of our lives...Let

74

us think, each and all, how we can best promote good First Communion. Priests, parents, religious sisters, teachers, devout and charitable laity—let all be persuaded that there are few works of religion and charity so dear to the heart of Jesus Christ as to instruct, but above all to watch, guard, civilise, and form to piety the souls of those who are in their first stage of the momentous journey of their life; of those who must live for ever or be for ever dead, according as they use the Eucharistic Communion of our Lord's Body, and on whose first and earliest partaking of that sovereign gift so signally depends each Communion of their lives—until that last one which ushers them into the presence of their Judge."[1]

Let us take to heart these solemn words and, in our own words, talk over affectionately and earnestly with the mothers we gather round us the best means of preparing for the great event in which we are all so deeply interested. Say that in the instructions now to be given the home-life of the Holy Child will be set before the children as the model of what a Christian home should be, and that they will be urged to imitate His reverence at prayer, His obedience, &c. Show how much a mother's intelligent help may do here. The child's will is weak. Watchful and loving care is needed to guide and second its efforts—prudence, too, and patience. We must not expect miracles at this time, or suppose that the prospect of the great day will so fill the volatile childish mind as to bring about the correction of every fault. Goodwill is about all we must expect. The child should know we look for this. But it would be a fatal mistake to make its faults at this time matter for special surprise and reproach. We must beware of exaggerated language in reprehending faults; for example, telling a child it has been very wicked indeed to tell a lie. Such words by

1   "Lenten Pastoral," 1893—Bishop Hedley.

forming a false conscience may do serious harm. Quietly and lovingly the mother should be noting the child's conduct and encouraging effort. Prayer morning and night, confession (more frequent, probably, during the time of preparation), punctuality at instructions—all these she should make her concern and forward as far as may be.

Say that a special resolution suggested to the children is that of being useful at home by helping mother. Point out the good that will come of efforts in this direction. How they will check the spirit of indolence, selfishness, and independence which nowadays bring sorrow into many a home. How they will interest the child in the details of home life, and foster a right sense of self-importance, as it notices how mother does this or that and is allowed to help her. Speak to them of the joy and comfort to the mother's heart such willing little hands and hearts may bring, and how useful a training will thus be provided for after years.

The mother will bear in mind it is the child's good that is the first consideration here, not the actual help afforded. She will look to the goodwill rather than to the service, give the little one credit for this, and show her appreciation of this if the hands are unskilful and the well-meant efforts mean extra work, and possibly mishaps. We all know the story of the child who, climbing the cupboard to reach a much-prized vase— because the flowers out of her own garden, long watched and watered for mother's birthday, would look so pretty in it—fell vase and all to the floor. And how the mother, coming in at the noise, severely reprehended the trembling child, making more account of a broken pot than of the motive which had prompted that loving little heart. Oh! what the mother lost that day. What a treasure of strengthened love and trust might have been hers had she but seen her opportunity and given praise and thanks and comfort instead of blame!

Let it not be said that the idea of usefulness at home supposes ideal conditions, and that our workers in the slums could only smile sadly at such an Utopian scheme. We know from the Reports of the National Society for the Prevention of Cruelty to Children that in the worst of homes, where positive brutality prevails, the friendly interest and remonstrance of the Society's officers score their triumphs each year. What is wanted is to get hold of the mothers, to make them feel the genuine interest we take in the comfort and happiness of their homes, and that it is in their power to aid us greatly in furthering this by the loving concern they will show in the efforts of their little children now. No doubt there are cases that resist every effort, but if a few homes could be bettered from the motive of helping a little child in its preparation at this time, would not all our endeavours have been well spent? Startling or immediate results are not to be looked for. But good example, like bad, is catching—and then for our encouragement we have the knowledge that it is God's cause we are forwarding, and that we have His help on which to count.

Family Prayer.—With a view to the home influence exercised at this time, plead if possible for the restoration amongst us of that reunion of the family at night, which was at one time a general practice in Catholic households? In days when the sanctity of the home is assailed in so many ways, and its safety and happiness need stronger defence than in the past, should we not do well to meet together at nightfall to secure a blessing and protection that will follow the children when they leave its shelter and enter on the battle of life? Experience shows that few impressions are earlier and more lasting than this—of seeing father, mother, brothers and sisters kneeling together as the day closes in united prayer. A young mother recently found her babe just three kneeling in a corner, the eyes closed, the little hands joined. To the question: "What are you doing, Pet?" came the reply: "I'se saying my prayers." "You see," explained the mother, "she had seen from her crib Jack and me saying our prayers together when he comes home of a night." Jack is a guard on the railway. Has he not had his reward already in the impression made where it will probably never be effaced!

No doubt when the habit of family prayer has been lost, effort is needed to recover it. But mothers are generous, and ready to use their influence here as far as prudence will allow. Plead with them to do what they can. If all the family cannot be gathered together for prayers at night, let the mother have the little ones with her and any others she can get. With fidelity and patience on her part the circle may grow. If at times she could not be present herself, an elder girl might take her place. Get them to make the effort to do what they can. Show them that the habit of morning and evening prayer is absolutely essential to perseverance in a Christian life. Would not God bless the determination to meet together for five minutes[1] each evening before the children go to bed, and thus let every member of the family help to train these little ones in the way they should go?

Congratulate the mothers on their power for good. Show them that, as a rule, children will be what their parents make them. What they learn at school will be strengthened or destroyed by what they see at home. Teachers may do their utmost, but parents have a duty towards their little ones which no one else can discharge. Whether they will or no, the child will learn its first and most lasting lessons *from them*. And what it sees will make a far greater impression than what it

1   The night prayers of the *Simple Prayer Book* (English Catholic Truth Society—one million two hundred thousand—price Id.) take no more than five minutes, examination of conscience included. [Editor's note: Mother Loyola utilized portions of the *Simple Prayer Book* in assembling her *Little Children's Prayer Book*.]

hears. Of what use is it for parents to have their children taught the duty of going to Mass on Sundays, of abstaining on Fridays, of going to the Sacraments regularly, of saying their prayers morning and night, if they fail in these duties themselves? Their example must bear out and enforce what is learned at school. And it is the mother's example and influence that tell most. It is in the mother's arms and on the mother's lap that the little child learns to lisp its first prayer, to learn the first lessons of its faith, to love Jesus in the crib, on the cross, in the tabernacle, to love the Blessed Mother of God. If it be true that what the child is in its sixth or seventh year, so it will remain, how great must be the responsibility of the mother during this important time. Show how saint after saint owes his holiness to the early training of a saintly mother, and that if we want to safeguard the innocence and the happiness of our children, we must first of all have good mothers.

Could we put these points before mothers with the earnestness born of deep conviction, could we bring them to look upon it as a privilege to help us now, what lasting fruits a First Communion might bring, not to the child alone, but to its home.

The Eve of First Communion

On the eve let the mothers see that the children get to bed in good time and that all is ready for the morrow. The dress should be festive, if possible, but simple, devoid of display, and of anything that could distract themselves or others.

The First Communion Day

The First Communicants should be in church at least ten minutes before Mass begins. Happy those that come accompanied by father and mother, and have them kneeling by them at the rails!

Let all at home help to make the great day as bright as possible. Let the children feel themselves the objects of reverent affection. Care should be taken that the presents, &c. be not over-exciting, and should there be Benediction in the evening all should attend.

On this point Cardinal Vaughan says :

"Let those who can, help by their zeal and kindness to impress upon the children that they have become for this momentous occasion objects of special care and delight. Hence the value of those little attentions which show themselves in the providing of even some small creature comforts, and gifts or loans, that help to make the great Feast-Day joyful and festive to these little people who are unaccustomed to have so much attention lavished upon them...We must in this matter conform to the nature of child-life and realise that the little lambs of the flock are to be taken according to their age and disposition...Where possible a simple breakfast might be prepared. Some suitable little memento such as a framed First Communion picture, a medal, a prayer-book, or other appropriate article might be given."

And again: "While a due recollection should be recommended, some special amusement may be provided for the children either on the day itself or on the next day. They should all be gathered together in the church some time during the day, to visit the Blessed Sacrament, and, if there be a procession, to walk in it all together, as the Children of the First Communion."[1]

AFTER FIRST COMMUNION

Now more than ever is the mother's care and influence indispensable to preserve in the heart of her child the happy fruits of its union with God. She must see that its prayers

---

1   *Synodus Diocesana Westmonasteriensis.* Anno 1902.

morning and night are said. She must watch over its reading, its companions, its amusements, keep out of her house the cheap novel, the sensational newspaper, borrowed hooks of which she knows nothing. Let her ascertain how often Confession and Communion are advised by the child's Confessor, and do what she can to see that its religious duties are faithfully fulfilled.

How often has it happened that in her zeal to promote her child's welfare a mother finds her own fervour quickened, that she begins to accompany the little one to the altar, and that the practice of frequent Communion thus gradually makes its way into a household!

On the other hand, how can we expect a child left to itself to keep up its fervour or form a habit of frequent Communion? It is not so much the First Communion as the second and those that follow which call for the solicitude of parents and teachers. The absence of the outward show that marked the great day can hardly fail to make a difference with children. So much is this the case, that some priests are averse to anything special in the way of dress on the First Communion day. But this seems to be going too far. Experience shows that some outward show is necessary. Children need all the help we can give them, and cannot afford to dispense with what appeals to the senses. "Even if we can do nothing more for them," says a Sister of Charity, "but lend them a white pinafore and give them their breakfast, it is a difference and makes an impression." When we think of the cheerless lives of some of these little creatures, when we hear of one going straight from the church, with its white rows of Communicants, its lights, and flowers, and song, to her miserable fireless home; of the mother not yet up, of the halfpenny thrown to her to get herself a bit of bread—we feel we must do what we can to brighten this greatest day in the life of a child, and make it stand out as a happy memory all life through.

The poverty of their everyday dress is a serious difficulty with our very poor children, and calls for friendly expostulation and encouragement. "Our Lord does not think about your hat," we must tell them. "If you haven't one, go to Him without; it is *yourself* He wants. On no account stay away from Him because you are poor. He was poor Himself and understands."

We must not leave our children suddenly and entirely to themselves once the First Communion day is over. To allow them the liberty granted by the Church of going to Communion as often as they wish, and at the same time to guard against the danger of letting a Communion depend on the whim of their waking moments, some priests tell the children to ask in each Confession for the number of times they want to go till their next Confession—*specifying the days.* An instruction in school on the Friday preceding the monthly Communion is a great help in maintaining fervour. Another help, and a motive for frequent Communion found to have great force with children, is the thought of our Lord, waiting in the tabernacle for each one of them, and the fear of disappointing Him if they stay away. "Oh, I did not think He would miss *me*," one child exclaimed in surprise, as this thought came home to her.

Those who see much of the poor tell us consoling things of the spiritual relish in receiving our Lord, often felt to a great degree by very young children. "The little lamp, and the little House on the altar where Jesus is" speak to these babes of realities hidden from the wise and prudent. Such relish and a keen sense of the help found in our Lord's Presence with them are an experience less common apparently with elder children.

What, then, we must encourage the little ones to form, is a habit of frequent Communion which will carry them safely through the critical years from thirteen to sixteen, known to those of wide experience as "the criminal stage of a child's life." The restraints of school life are over, and often, alas, the restraints of home-life are broken through. Girls of thirteen or fourteen will leave home, try to live in lodgings on their earnings of half-a-crown a week, and only when something big happens find out that they have made a mistake and ought to be by their mother's side at home.

Every effort must be made to strengthen the ties of home and thus protect our children from the spirit of independence which is the ruin of so many. The time of preparation for First Communion should have this effect among others. The little ones will be taught now to make themselves useful at home, to show their love for mother by helping her in every way they can. And to mothers we would say: "Love them. *Make them feel you love them.* Make them love you and home very much. Try to keep up this love all their lives through. It will help the children and help you, and next to the holy influences of their religion, will be a power for good that neither time nor trial will weaken."

XII

Summing Up

We hope it will not be considered an unpardonable presumption if we do this in the weighty words of the Synodal Allocution, to which we have more than once referred; and in the words of Cardinal Vaughan's Lenten Letter of 1903.

"The most important religious event in a child's life is undoubtedly the First Communion. Very frequently it turns out to be the most important in the whole of a long and chequered career. How often has the soul returned to God upon a death-bed through the memory of the First Communion! It was the one great religious act that had impressed itself indelibly on the heart. Nothing had altogether effaced the memory of the grace received in a First Communion which had been thoroughly well prepared for.

The Church fully recognises this fact, and therefore her desire everywhere and her practice in all Catholic countries has been to make much of the preparation of children for their First Communion. As an experienced and prudent mother she fortifies them against the coming dangers and storms of life by giving to them the Bread of the Strong which is our Lord Himself come down from Heaven. She desires that the first solemn entry of His Divine Majesty into their souls should be like the first entry of a king into his city or kingdom, which is preceded by great popular preparations, and is accompanied by special manifestations of joyful honour and respect. It is a thing never to be forgotten by those who take the principal part in it."[1]

"To train children effectively the priests and the catechists must make use of such means and industries as are best calculated to interest them. They must get hold not only of their reason, but of their imagination, of their affections and their will, of their innocent inclinations and tastes; and steadily enlist all these on the side of their true and everlasting happiness.

Simply to learn the Catechism by heart, like the multiplication table, will never mould their character. Unless the doctrines of religion are duly prepared and seasoned to their taste and appetite, unless they are assimilated by *all the powers of the soul*, they will, like undigested food, occasion discomfort and disgust rather than pleasure and satisfaction."[2]

Among the practical suggestions of the Letter to parents and catechists are the following:—

"1. Illustrate well all your Catechism lessons, and the children will love them. Interesting stories, read or told from the Old and New Testaments, from Church History and Saints' Lives, will rivet and fascinate their attention.[3]

2. Good coloured prints and pictures that tell parts of a story are wonderful helps. The eye lights up the imagination, and the imagination is the picture-book of the mind. Explain and point out the details in the picture, and sometimes let

1 *Synodus Diocesana Westmonasteriensis.* Anno 1902. p. 14.
2 Lenten Letter on the Religious Training of Children, 1903—Cardinal Vaughan.
3 We recommend Gibson's "Catechism made Easy," in two vols., price 3s. 9d.—Burns & Oates. It is full of examples and short stories, and will make teaching easy, even to those that have but little experience.

a child explain the pictures to the whole class. The magic lantern might also be used in connection with explanations of Catechism and religion, even in Church, where proper arrangements can be made.[1]...

4. Especially make the children sing. St. Francis Xavier used to make them sing their prayers and even the Catechism... And Father Furniss, the most fascinating catechist we have had in England, depended almost entirely on singing the Catechism in verse and appropriate hymns, in addition to stories, anecdotes, and appeals to the imagination. Our own venerable Bede, in a letter to Archbishop Egbert in the eighth century, says that "in order to make instruction *sink deeper into their hearts*, they should be taught not only to say, but carefully *to sing* their prayers—the Our Father, and the Apostles' Creed, &c. One great advantage of singing is that it gives more time to think of the meaning of the words. Hurry is in reciting—not in singing.

5. Some people are for ever correcting children, but never praise or reward them. Be firm, be the master, and punish if need be, but give plenty of praise and encouragement. Often bestow tokens of approval—little presents of no money value. Better these than costly gifts, because you want the child to value the approval rather than the token, and expensive presents must be rare. The Catholic Truth Society can supply the need. St. Francis of Sales used to carry about medals, rosaries, pious pictures, and such things to give to children who answered their Catechism well, or who pleased him by their good conduct; and, strange as it may appear, grave Ecclesiastical Councils have decreed that churches must furnish little rewards to give away as encouragement to good children.

6. The system of giving marks to children at every class for

---

1   Schnorr's very artistic coloured prints, forty-five in number, of the Old and New Testaments, can now be obtained from the Catholic Truth Society.

knowledge and for good conduct, and rewarding those who obtain a maximum of good marks at the end of the month by some little prize publicly bestowed, is very effective. Prizes, distinctions, precedencies, and other forms of approbation should be freely used. A little emulation awakens the faculties and keeps a whole class on the alert.

Do not grown-up people, civilians, and soldiers covet a clasp, a medal, a ribbon, letters appended, and titles prefixed to their name? Sovereigns seem unable to satisfy the demand. Children also have the same appetite, which is an instinct of our nature, and are led by it. Encouragement stimulates and brightens, and it is enhanced by being given publicly.

Again, to give children a treat, to take them for an excursion to play a game, to visit a church, an altar, a convent, or a gallery, to get up an entertainment for them and their parents—all these things signify affection, esteem, real charity, and have a magical power to make children bright and happy, and associate the thought of their religion with genial and pleasant memories.

7. One more word to parents and catechists. If you wish the children to he bright and interested, be bright and interested yourself. If you teach a lesson, tell a story, exhibit a picture, show that you yourself enter with spirit into the matter. Let all see that you can be moved to indignation, to admiration, to love. Do not hesitate to lead your hearers to pray. A catechist, like a preacher, must exhibit by words, tone, gesture, his own faith and feeling if he would make his hearers believe and feel aright. Feeling of admiration, fear, hatred, desire, love are catching. Children are delightfully simple and responsive to earnestness."[1]

Our talks end as they began, with a word of pleading. We must reanimate our faith as to the grandeur of the work

1   Lenten Letter as above.

entrusted to us, its responsibility, and the supernatural motives which should inspire all our labour. As God's instruments, it behoves us to be closely united to the Divine Hand. If He is to influence others through us He must first direct ourselves. The conviction that only out of our own fullness can we hope to be helpful to others, will prove a powerful stimulus to efforts after personal holiness. "For them do I sanctify Myself" (St. John xvii. 19), are our Lord's own words—wonderful on His lips—and a motto for every teacher.

Additional titles available from

St. Augustine Academy Press

Books for the Traditional Catholic

Titles by Mother Mary Loyola:

Blessed are they that Mourn
Confession and Communion
Coram Sanctissimo (Before the Most Holy)
First Communion
First Confession
Forgive us our Trespasses
Hail! Full of Grace
Heavenwards
Holy Mass/How to Help the Sick and Dying
Home for Good
Jesus of Nazareth: The Story of His Life Written for Children
The Child of God: What comes of our Baptism
The Children's Charter
The Little Children's Prayer Book
The Soldier of Christ: Talks before Confirmation
Welcome! Holy Communion Before and After

Tales of the Saints:

A Child's Book of Saints by William Canton
A Child's Book of Warriors by William Canton
Illustrated Life of the Blessed Virgin by Rev. B. Rohner, O.S.B.
Legends & Stories of Italy by Amy Steedman
Mary, Help of Christians by Rev. Bonaventure Hammer
The Book of Saints and Heroes by Lenora Lang
Saint Patrick: Apostle of Ireland
The Story of St. Elizabeth of Hungary by William Canton

Check our Website for more:

www.staugustineacademypress.com

CPSIA information can be obtained
at www.ICGtesting.com
Printed in the USA
FSHW021350240620
71377FS

9 781936 639052